COME AND SEE

Catholic Bible Study

Moses and the Torah
Exodus, Leviticus, Numbers, Deuteronomy

by

Fr. Joseph Ponessa, S.S.D.

and

Laurie Watson Manhardt, Ph.D.

Emmaus Road Publishing
827 North Fourth Street
Steubenville, OH 43952

All rights reserved. Published in 2007
Printed in the United States of America

Library of Congress Control Number: 2007925020
ISBN: 978-1-931018-45-6

Cover design and layout by
Jacinta Caluct, Image Graphics & Design www.image–gd.com

Cover artwork:
Melissa Dayton, Moses and the Burning Bush
www.pearlsofgracefineart.com

Nihil obstat: Monsignor Joseph N. Rosie, *Censor Librorum*
Imprimatur: Most Reverend John M. Smith, Bishop of Trenton
May 9, 2007

The *nihil obstat* and *imprimatur* are official declarations
that a book is free of doctrinal or moral error.

For additional information on the "Come and See ~ Catholic Bible Study"
series visit www.CatholicBibleStudy.net

Come and See

Catholic Bible Study

Moses and the Torah
Exodus, Leviticus, Numbers, Deuteronomy

Introduction

Who is like thee, O Lord, among the gods?
Who is like thee, majestic in holiness, terrible in glorious deeds, doing wonders.
Exodus 15:11

To the Jews, the first five books of the Bible are the most important because they have the authority of Moses, who is their most important prophet and teacher. The first five books of the Old Testament (Hebrew Bible)—Genesis, Exodus, Leviticus, Numbers, Deuteronomy—are called by the name Pentateuch, which comes from the Greek word *Pentateuchos*, meaning "a book of five scrolls." The Jews call these books *ha-Torah*, which is Hebrew for "The Law."

Moses is the most imposing figure of the Old Testament because of the miracles that were wrought through him—the burning bush, the plagues, and the parting of the Red Sea, and also because he is the one who spoke with God. So, the Torah is the testimony of Moses, and what he heard God say, and what he did by the power of God. Whereas, for the Christian, the Gospels are the testimony of what the apostles learned through Jesus, and the miracles He worked in their midst.

The Pentateuch details God's revelation concerning creation, and describes the formation of the People of God starting with the patriarchs: Abraham, Isaac, and Jacob. Genesis, the first book of the Bible, has been covered in an entire *"Come and See ~ Catholic Bible Study"* book in this series. You might want to simply review the book of Genesis in your Bible before beginning this study. Genesis provides the background for the story of the chosen people, who are in bondage in Egypt.

At the beginning of the book of Exodus, the figure of Moses is presented. *Exodus* comes from the Greek word for "departure" or going out. Moses leads the people of Israel in their departure from the slavery of Egypt, across the Red Sea, to the dessert, and finally, to freedom found in the Promised Land. Along the way, God reveals His name and His glory to Moses and presents His law to Moses on Mount Sinai. Despite the faithfulness of God, the people prove to be repeatedly unfaithful.

Since God desires to dwell among His people, they must be holy. In Leviticus, Moses, the great lawgiver, gives laws pertaining to ritual holiness, sacrifices, and legal purity. God expects His people to be holy, because He is holy.

Numbers recounts two censuses of the Hebrew people, with legal ordinances and history interspersed. Here, God also punishes the murmurings of His people.

Deuteronomy is a type of second law, in which Moses repeats and explains the original laws, and then gives more directives to the people. At the end of Deuteronomy, Moses' last word and testament are given to the people before his death, and prior to their entry into the Promised Land.

What You Need

To do this Bible Study, you will need a Catholic Bible, and a *Catechism of the Catholic Church* (CCC). When choosing a Bible, remember that the Catholic Bible contains 73 books. If you find Sirach and Tobit in your Bible's table of contents, you have a complete Catholic Bible. The Council of Hippo approved these 73 books in AD 393, and this has remained the official canon of Sacred Scripture since the Fourth Century. The Council of Trent in AD 1545 authoritatively reaffirmed these divinely inspired books for inclusion in the canon of the Bible. The Douay-Rheims, one of the first English translations of the Catholic Bible, was completed in AD 1609.

For bible study purposes, choose a word-for-word, literal translation rather than a paraphrase. Some excellent translations are the Revised Standard Version Catholic Edition (RSVCE), the Jerusalem Bible (JB), and the New American Bible (NAB).

How To Do This Bible Study

1. Pray to the Holy Spirit to enlighten your mind and spirit.
2. Read the bible passages for the first chapter.
3. Read the commentary in this book.
4. Use your Bible and Catechism to write answers to the home study questions.
5. Find a small group and share your answers aloud on those questions.
6. Watch the videotape lecture that goes with this study.
7. End with a short wrap-up lecture and/or prayer.

Invite and Welcome Priests and Religious

Ask for the blessing of your pastor before you begin. Invite your pastor, associate pastor, deacon, visiting priests, and religious sisters to participate in bible study. Invite priests and religious to come and pray with the bible study members, periodically answer questions from the question box, or give a wrap-up lecture. Accept whatever they can offer to the bible study. However, don't expect or demand anything from them. Appreciate that the clergy are very busy and don't add additional burdens. Accept with gratitude whatever is offered.

Practical Considerations

❋ Ask God for wisdom about whom to study with, where, and when to meet.
❋ Gather a small prayer group to pray for your bible study and your specific needs. Pray to discern God's will in your particular situation.

* Show this book to your pastor and ask for his approval and direction.
* Choose a day of the week and time to meet.
* Invite neighbors and friends to a "Get Acquainted Coffee" to find out who will make a commitment to meet for 60 to 90 minutes each week for bible study.
* Find an appropriate location. Start in someone's home or in the parish hall if the space is available and the pastor will allow it.
* Hire a babysitter for mothers with young children and share the cost amongst everyone, or find some volunteers to provide childcare.
* Consider a cooperative arrangement, in which women take turns caring for the children. All women, even grandmothers and women without children, should take turns, serving the children as an offering to God.

Pray that God will anoint specific people to lead your study. Faithful, practicing Catholics are needed to fill the following positions:

* **Teachers** – take responsibility to read commentaries and prepare a fifteen to twenty minute wrap-up lecture after the small group discussion and video.
* **Song Leaders** – lead everyone in singing a short hymn to begin bible study.
* **Prayer Leaders** – open bible study with a short prayer.
* **Children's Teachers** – teach the young children who come to bible study.
* **Coordinators** – communicate with parish personnel about needs for rooms, microphones, and video equipment. Make sure rooms are left in good shape.
* **Small Group Facilitators** will be needed for each small group. Try to enlist two mature Catholics who are good listeners to serve together as co-leaders for each small group and share the following responsibilities:

    ❖ Pray for each member of your small group every day.
    ❖ Make a nametag for each member of the group.
    ❖ Meet before the study to pray with other leaders.
    ❖ Discuss all the questions in the lesson each week.
    ❖ Begin and end on time.
    ❖ Make sure that each person in the group shares each week. Ask each person to read a question and have the first chance to answer it.
    ❖ In the discussion group go around in a circle, so each person looks forward to his or her turn to read a question. After reading the question, the reader can answer the question or pass, and then others can feel free to add additional comments.
    ❖ Make sure that no one person dominates the discussion, including you!

    ❖ Keep the discussion positive and focused on the week's lesson.
    ❖ Speak kindly and charitably. Steer conversation away from any negative or uncharitable speech, gossip, or griping. Don't badmouth anyone or any church.
    ❖ Listen well! Keep your ears open and your eyes on the person speaking.
    ❖ Give your full attention to the one speaking. Be comfortable with silence. Be patient. Encourage quieter people to share first. Ask questions.

❖ If questions, misunderstandings, or disagreements arise, refer them to the question box for a teacher to research or the parish priest to answer later.
❖ Arrange for a social activity each month.

Practical Considerations

✳ Jesus chose a group of twelve apostles. So, perhaps twelve or thirteen people make the best small groups. When you get too many, break into two groups.
✳ A group of teenagers or a young adult group could be facilitated by the parish priest or a young adult leader.
✳ Men share best with men and women with women. If you have a mixed bible study, organize separate men's groups led by men and women's groups led by women. In mixed groups, some people tend to remain silent.
✳ Offer a married couples' group, if two married couples are willing to lead the group. Each person should have his or her own book.

✳ Sit next to the most talkative person in the group and across from the quietest. Use eye contact to affirm and encourage quieter people to speak up. Serve everyone and hear from everyone.
✳ Listening in bible study is just as important as talking. Evaluate each week. Did everyone share? Am I a good listener? Did I really hear what others shared? Was I attentive or distracted? Did I affirm others? Did I talk too much?
✳ Share the overall goal aloud with all of the members of the group. The goal is to hear from each person in the group, sharing aloud each time the group meets.
✳ Make sure that people share answers only on those questions on which they have written down answers. Don't just share off the top of your head. Really study.

✳ Consider a nursing mothers' group in which mothers can bring their infants and hold them while sharing their home study questions.
✳ Family groups can work together on a family bible study night, reading the commentary and scriptures aloud and helping one another to find answers in the Bible and Catechism.
✳ Parents or older siblings can read to young children and help the youngsters to do the crafts in the children's bible study book.

Social Activities

God has created us as social creatures, needing to relate communally. Large parishes make it difficult for people to get to know one another. Some people can belong to a parish for years without getting to know others. Newcomers may never get noticed and welcomed. Bible study offers an opportunity for spiritual nourishment as well as inclusion and hospitality. Occasional social activities are recommended in this book.

These socials are simple, fun, and easy. In planning your social activities be meek and docile to the Holy Spirit and try to attend with your group.

❋ Agree on a time when most of the group can meet. This could be right before or after bible study or a different day of the week, perhaps even Saturday morning.
❋ Invite people to come to your home for the social time. Jesus was comfortable visiting the homes of the rich and the poor. So, whatever your circumstances, as a Christian you can offer hospitality to those God sends along your way.

"Do not neglect to show hospitality to strangers,
for thereby some have entertained angels unawares."
(Hebrews 13:2)

❋ Keep it simple! Just a beverage and cookies work well. Simplicity blesses others. People can squeeze together on a sofa or stand around the kitchen. Don't fuss.
❋ Help the group leader. If bible study meets in someone's home, invite the group to come to your place for the social time. Don't make the group leader do it all.
❋ If bible study meets at church, don't have all of the socials at church as well. Try to have some fellowship times in people's homes. Perhaps over the Christmas break you can go to someone's home for coffee and cookies after Christmas and before bible study starts up again.

Suggested Times for Socials

9:30–10:30 a.m.	Saturday coffee	12:00–1:00 p.m.	Luncheon
3:00–4:00 p.m.	Afternoon tea	8:00–9:00 p.m.	Dessert

Modify times to meet your specific needs. If your parish has Saturday morning Mass at 9:00 a.m., adjust the time of your social to accommodate those members of the group who would like to attend Mass and need some time to get to the social. If lunch after bible study makes too long of a day for children who need naps, plan the social for a different day. A mother's group might meet after school when high school students are available to baby-sit.

Class Schedule

Accept responsibility for being a good steward of time. God gives each of us twenty-four hours every day. If bible study starts or ends late, busy people may drop out. Late starts punish the prompt and encourage tardiness. Be a good steward of time. Begin and end bible study with prayer at the agreed upon time. If people consistently arrive late or leave early, investigate whether you have chosen the best time for most people. You may have a conflict with the school bus schedule or the parish Mass schedule. Perhaps beginning a few minutes earlier or later could be a service to those mothers who need to pick up children from school.

Possible Bible Study Class Schedules

Morning Class

9:30 a.m.	Welcome, song, prayer
9:40 a.m.	Video
9:55 a.m.	Small group discussion
10:40 a.m.	Wrap-up lecture and prayer

Afternoon Class

1:00 p.m.	Welcome, song, prayer
1:10 p.m.	Small group discussion
1:55 p.m.	Video
2:10 p.m.	Wrap-up lecture and prayer

Evening Class

7:30 p.m.	Welcome, song, prayer
7:40 p.m.	Small group discussion
8:25 p.m.	Video
8:40 p.m.	Wrap-up lecture and prayer

As you can see, the video could be shown either before or after the small group discussion, and either before, after, or instead of a wrap-up lecture. Whether or not you choose to use the videotapes, please begin and end with prayer.

Wrap-Up Lecture

Father Ponessa provides additional information in videotaped lectures, which are available for this study and can be obtained from Emmaus Road Publishing Company, 827 North Fourth Street, Steubenville, Ohio, 43952. You can obtain DVDs or videocassettes of these lectures by going to www.emmausroad.org on the Internet or by calling 1-800-398-5470. Videotaped lectures may be used in addition to, or in place of a wrap-up lecture, depending on your needs.

When offering a closing lecture, the presenter should spend extra time in prayer and study to prepare a good, sound lecture. The lecturer should consult several Catholic bible study commentaries and prepare a cohesive, orthodox lecture. Several members of the leaders' team could take turns giving wrap-up lectures. Also, invite priests, deacons, and religious sisters to give an occasional lecture.

The lecturer should:
* Be a faithful, practicing Catholic. Seek spiritual direction. Frequent the sacraments, especially the Eucharist and Reconciliation.
* Obtain the approval and blessing of your parish priest to teach.
* Use several different presenters whenever possible.
* Pray daily for all of the leaders and members of the study.
* Pray over the lesson to be studied and presented.

* Outline the bible passages to be studied.
* Identify the main idea of the bible study lesson.
* Find a personal application from the lesson. How can one make a practical response to God's word?
* Plan a wrap-up lecture with a beginning, a middle, and an end.
* Use index cards to keep focused. Don't read your lecture; talk to people.

* Proclaim, teach, and reiterate the teachings of the Catholic Church. Learn what the Catholic Church teaches, and proclaim the fullness of truth.
* Illustrate the main idea presented in the passage by using true stories from the lives of the saints, or the lives of contemporary Christians.
* Use visuals—a flip chart or overhead transparencies if possible.
* Plan a skit, act out a bible story, and interact with the group.

* Try to make the scriptures come alive for the people in your group.
* Provide a question box. Find answers to difficult questions or ask a parish priest to come and answer questions on occasion.
* When difficult or complex personal problems arise or are shared in the group, seek out the counsel of a priest.
* Begin and end on time. When you get to the end of your talk, stop and pray.

Challenges

"All scripture is inspired by God and profitable for teaching, for reproof, for correction, and for training in righteousness, that the man of God may be complete, equipped for every good work" (2 Timothy 3:16-17).

As Christians, all of us are weak and need God's mercy and forgiveness. Lay groups can attract people with problems and challenges. Don't try to be all things for all people.

Jesus is the Savior, and we are only His servants. When problems loom, direct them to a priest or counselor. Bible study demands faithfulness to the task at hand, while praying for others and their needs. Saint Paul encourages us to "speak the truth in love … and be kind to one another, tenderhearted, forgiving one another, as God in Christ forgave you" (Ephesians 4:15,32). Bible study provides the opportunity for us to search God's word for direction in our personal lives and to pray for, encourage, and sometimes gently admonish one another.

The words "God said" appear ten times in the creation account. In this way the creation narrative anticipates the Ten Commandments. This makes us realize that these Ten Commandments are, as it were, an echo of the creation; they are not arbitrary inventions for the purpose of erecting barriers to human freedom but signs pointing to the spirit, the language, and the meaning of creation; they are a translation of the language of the universe, a translation of God's logic, which constructed the universe. …

Creation is designed in such a way that it is oriented to worship. It fulfills its purpose and assumes its significance when it is lived, ever new, with a view to worship. …

In the creation account the Sabbath is depicted as the day when the human being, in the freedom of worship, participates in God's freedom, in God's rest, and thus in God's peace. To celebrate the Sabbath means to celebrate the covenant. It means to return to the source and to sweep away all the defilement that our work has brought with it. It also means going forth into a new world in which there will no longer be slaves and masters but only free children of God. …

Each human being is known by God and loved by him. Each is willed by God, and each is God's image. Precisely in this consists the deeper and greater unity of human-kind—that each of us, each individual human being, realizes the one project of God and has his or her origin in the same creative idea of God. Hence the Bible says that whoever violates a human being, violates God's property…

Pope Benedict XVI (Cardinal Ratzinger), *In the Beginning*
(Grand Rapids, MI: Eerdmans, 1995), pp. 26, 27, 30–31, 45.

A Prayer to the Holy Spirit

O Holy Spirit, Beloved of my soul, I adore You,
enlighten, guide, strengthen and console me.
Tell me what I ought to say and do, and command me to do it.
I promise to be submissive in everything You will ask of me
and to accept all that You permit to happen to me,
only show me what is Your will.

Chapter 1

Moses in Egypt
Exodus 1–2

**She took pity on him and said,
"This is one of the Hebrews' children."**
Exodus 2:6b

In the days of Moses, Egypt was indisputably the greatest country in the world, with the largest territory, the longest history, and the strongest economy. Peace reigned the full length of the country, from the Nile delta in the north, down nearly as far as Ethiopia. For nearly two thousand years, with only a few interruptions, the Egyptians had enjoyed a strong central government. The Nile valley produced huge wheat harvests, a high-protein durum wheat which nourished the Egyptians themselves and also provided an important export commodity.

The Book of Genesis, the first of the five books of Moses, the Torah, focuses our attention on two nations, Egypt, and Israel. These two nations had the same ancestral roots. Noah had three sons—Shem, Ham, and Japheth (Genesis 5:32). Shem was the father of the Semites, among whom are the Hebrews; Ham was the father of the Hamites, who include the Egyptians (Genesis 10). This connection of Israel and Egypt continued. The Hebrew patriarchs moved westwards and ventured down into Egypt. In a time of famine, Abraham and Sarah went down into Egypt (Genesis 12:10), and decades later, in another time of famine, their grandson Jacob settled there with his sons and flocks (Geneses 46:6–7). Abraham's great-grandson Joseph even became a high official, administrator of the country in the name of Pharaoh (Genesis 41:44). By the end of the Book of Genesis, the Egyptians and Hebrews have become two peoples occupying a single land. But the descendants of Israel were more fruitful (Exodus 1:7).

As shepherds, the Hebrews settled not in the agricultural land of the Nile valley, but on the edge of the delta region. Their flocks could still pasture in dry land, but they also ate the straw from the Egyptian wheat crop, stalks of wheat discarded after the harvesting of the grain. This fodder was stored for use throughout the year. Hence, the flocks of the Hebrews prospered, and with them the people. In Egypt the Hebrews, fulfilling God's first command to the human race (Genesis 1:28) experienced blessing and fertility.

The Hebrews dwelt in a frontier region, the land of Goshen (Exodus 8:22). Four centuries before, a foreign people, the Hyksos, had invaded from that direction bringing an end to the Egyptian Middle Kingdom period, and for a while ruled the Nile delta area. Thus, the Egyptians kept an eye on that border, fearful that another group of barbarians might try to do the same thing. In fact, after the lapse of many centuries, the Persians, then, the Greeks, and later yet, the Romans entered Egypt from the northeast, just as the Hyksos had done. For this reason, the growing Hebrew presence made the Pharaoh and his government nervous.

While they were just a small clan related to the important royal administrator Joseph, the Hebrews were welcome guests in the land of Egypt. Around the time of Joseph, the Pharaoh Akhenaten abolished the worship of many gods and instituted the worship of the one God in Egypt. Possibly the presence of the Hebrews was an inspiration for that revolutionary period in Egyptian history. Counter-revolutionary forces rolled back the Akhenaten reforms after his death, however, and that too may have been a factor in making the Hebrews less welcome.

"Now there arose a new king over Egypt" (Exodus 1:8). The author of Exodus sometimes refers to the ruler of Egypt as "king" and sometimes as "pharaoh," but never by his own proper name. That makes it difficult to determine how many rulers appear in the course of the narrative. The mention of a new king in verse eight hints at a change of dynasty. Soon after the death of Akhenaten, the Eighteenth Dynasty ended, and an assertive new family came to the throne. Ramesses I ruled just a year, but his son Seti I reigned long enough to solidify the family's hold on power, and then his son Ramesses II had one of the longest reigns in all Egyptian history.

These no-nonsense rulers of the Nineteenth Dynasty had to decide what to do with the Hebrews. They could either expel them from the land, or incorporate them into the Egyptian way of life. Expulsion was dangerous, for the Hebrews could then return as military foes. So the rulers decided on a policy of integration. Egyptians worked in the field for six months of the year, but during the annual flooding of the Nile, they were conscripted for public works projects, like building pyramids. By the time of Exodus, the last pyramid had already been built. So, the new monarchs enlist the Hebrew population in the project of building a new capital city called Pi-Ramesse.

The Hebrews could not adapt very well to their new duties. They were a pastoral people, with flocks of sheep and goats requiring attention year-round. They could not leave their flocks for six months, and then return to find the livestock healthy and thriving. Integration of the Hebrews into the Egyptian state economy meant ripping them out of their pastoral context altogether. The Hebrews were reduced from the status of prosperous shepherds, with year-round independence of life-style, to poverty-stricken slave laborers. Nevertheless, they continued to multiply in the land, so Pharaoh turned to population control, in one of the earliest known examples of human genocide. The Hebrews were too dangerous to expel and too rebellious to integrate, so the king turned to infanticide as his final solution.

"Why have you done this" (Exodus 1:18)? Only fifteen verses into the Book of Exodus, two heroines appear, midwives who helped the Hebrew women in childbirth. They are the first named characters to appear in this book. Their names are *Shiprah*, which means "beauty," and *Puah*, which means "splendor." Perhaps these are nicknames, and not their real names. Very likely these are Egyptian women with Egyptian names, which the Hebrew women may have found difficult to pronounce. The Hebrew women gave the midwives gracious, honorary Hebrew titles in gratitude for the service they rendered. They practice already, before the time of Hippocrates, the Hippocratic oath taken by doctors, to do no harm. They are great heroines of the Exodus story, the first so-called "righteous gentiles" who saved Jewish lives during pogrom and persecution. This demonstrates that many Egyptians had good moral values, despite the wickedness of their government.

Frustrated by his failure to suppress the Hebrew birth rate surreptitiously, Pharaoh orders his subjects to cast all Hebrew male babies into the river. Instead of leaving the manner of death to one's discretion, Pharaoh commands drowning. In the Egyptian religion, death by drowning in the Nile was seen as a special honor. Temples were built along the riverbank to honor as gods those who had drowned. The Nile was a sacred river, and the Egyptian funeral ceremony had a boat ride across the Nile from the land of the living on the East Bank, to the land of the dead on the West Bank. So Pharaoh may have intended some kind of sick honor to the Hebrew baby boys by having them thrown into the Nile, unlike Herod who killed the baby boys of Bethlehem by the sword.

Government mandated population control has a long, terrible history associated with racism, sexism, and genocide. In Communist China, couples are allowed only one child and there is forced abortion. Girl babies are often aborted, now producing a crisis for young men of marriageable age who cannot find young Chinese women to marry. Minorities and poor people are especially vulnerable. Family planning can be a form of genocide directed against unwanted social or racial groups. The state that attempts to dictate birth control places itself in direct opposition to God's command to multiply and fill the earth.

The killing of an innocent child is the most heinous form of homicide. The murder of an adult is the wrongful end of a life partially lived, but the murder of a child prevents a life that could and would have been. The Jewish Talmud states: "One who saves a life saves the universe." The Koran quotes that verse with approval. So, Jews, Christians, and Muslims should all be affirming and protecting life.

Then Pharaoh commanded all the people, "Every son that is born to the Hebrews you shall cast into the Nile, but you shall let every daughter live." (Exodus 1:22)	He sent and killed all the male children in Bethlehem and in all that region who were two years old or under, according to the time he had ascertained from the wise men. (Matthew 2:16b)

The devil wanted to prevent Moses, and later, Jesus from appearing on the face of the earth. So, the devil influenced governments to subject an entire population to infanticide in the vain attempt to thwart God's plan. The babies who died instead of Baby Jesus are called the Holy Innocents. Perhaps the same designation could be extended to those who died instead of baby Moses.

> …Careful consideration should be given to the danger of this power (of population control) passing into the hands of those public authorities who care little for the precepts of moral law.
>
> Pope Paul VI, *Humanae Vitae* (1968), 17.
>
> The inviolability of the innocent human being's right to life "from the moment of conception to natural death" is a sign and requirement of the very inviolability of the person to whom the Creator has given the gift of life. … The human being must be respected—as a person—from the very first instant of his existence.
> Congregation for the Doctrine of the Faith, *Donum Vitae* (February 27, 1987), I, 4.
>
> *No human lawgiver can assert: it is permissible for you to kill, you have the right to kill, or you should kill.* Tragically, in the history of our century this has occurred when political forces have come to power, even by democratic means, and have passed laws contrary to the right to life of every human being.
>
> Pope John Paul II, *Letter to Families* (1994), 21.

A similar disregard for innocent human life that was present in the mind of pharaoh so many centuries ago, continues in the minds of some people today, who hold certain lives to be inconvenient and expendable.

"Now a man from the house of Levi took to wife a daughter of Levi" (Exodus 2:1). The fact that this is a priestly family is important, because they belong to what will become the tribe of the Levitical priesthood. The author specifies the tribal affiliation of this man's wife, because in Jewish law, a child belongs to the mother's tribe. This verse shows that the person about to be born, Moses, will belong to the tribe of Levi through the maternal line. Other details of family history evolve later.

It is not until Exodus 6:20 that the names of the couple are revealed. Moses' father's name is Amram, son of Kohath, son of Levi, and his mother's name is Jochebed, the daughter of Levi. In Exodus 2, a daughter is born, but not until Exodus 15:20, do we learn that her name is Miriam.

Exodus 4:14 reveals that the couple has two sons, not only the one who is put into the river, Moses, but another son, named Aaron, as well. Later yet, we learn that Aaron is three years older than his brother, because when Aaron is eighty-three, his brother is eighty (Exodus 7:7). The difference in age explains why Aaron was not put in a basket, because he was already old enough to be exempt from the law.

This method of disclosing information piece meal may be frustrating to modern readers, who like to have their facts served to them in sequence. The original readers of the Book of Exodus, however, already knew these facts well. The book existed to refresh already existing knowledge. As one grows in biblical literacy, the ancient method of narration becomes more comprehensible.

"She took pity on him" (Exodus 2:6b). Just as the midwives were heroines earlier, so Pharaoh's daughter is also a heroine. Her own father had issued the awful decree that everyone in the land should kill Hebrew boy babies, and yet she takes pity on this little one. She is a strong woman, with a good conscience. No one, not even her royal father, could make her violate her sense of right and duty. A world inhabited by women such as this would be a wonderful place.

There were many strong women among the royal families of Egypt. Several women took the throne and ruled in their own name, most notably Hatshepsut of the Eighteenth Dynasty. Nefertiti, the wife of Pharaoh Akhenaten, appears together with him in a number of paintings, and the naturalistic type of art of the time reveals her amazing beauty alongside his physical deformity. At the very time of Exodus, another queen, Nefertari, had a notable presence in the land alongside her husband, Pharaoh Ramesses II. Temples were built in her honor, but never as large as those honoring her husband.

In Exodus, the Egyptians are never painted as the enemy. Pharaoh may have hardened his heart against the Hebrews, but Pharaoh's people are not portrayed as hard-hearted. One young Egyptian noblewoman of good will and strong moral fiber saved a baby's life, and that baby led a whole nation into freedom. That woman made possible the salvation of Israel.

"She named him Moses" (Exodus 2:10). We know the greatest prophet of Israel by the name Moses, which is an Egyptian name. The author of Exodus gives the next best thing to a Hebrew etymology with *Moshe* "I drew him out of the water" (Exodus 2:10), but Pharaoh's daughter is the one speaking. In fact, a form of this name was very common among pharaohs of that time. During the Eighteenth Dynasty four pharaohs were named Tut-Moses. During the Nineteenth and Twentieth Dynasties, thirteen pharaohs were called Ra-Moses or Ramesses. *Tut* and *Ra* are gods in the Egyptian pantheon, and when used as a prefix with Moses, mean "Born of Ra" or "Born of Tut."

Moses certainly had another Hebrew name which his natural mother used during the years when she served as his wet-nurse. That name is lost to history. In fact, the Egyptians probably called him Ramesses or something like that. Thus the name Moses, may be a compromise between a lost Hebrew name and a longer Egyptian name. Moses belonged to two nations, but felt fully at home in neither.

"An Egyptian delivered us" (Exodus 2:19). The Midianites thought they were being saved by an Egyptian! Because Moses had been saved from reprehensible government ordered population control, he lived to save others. The Hebrews, in the bondage of slavery, cried out to God for deliverance. One who had been delivered was chosen to deliver them. Moses' two mothers, his natural Hebrew mother and his adoptive Egyptian mother, both imparted their value systems to him. Moses represents the best of Egypt as well as of Israel. Both nations deserve to claim him proudly.

1. List the twelve sons of Israel.

Genesis 35:22–25	Exodus 1:1–5

2. Who came up into Egypt? Genesis 46:8–27

3. Identify some reasons that Jacob went to Egypt.

Genesis 41:54–57	
Genesis 45:25–28	
Genesis 46:1–5	

4. What problem did the new king of Egypt identify? Exodus 1:7–9

5. Describe the promise to Abraham fulfilled by God.

Genesis 22:17	
Deuteronomy 10:22	

6. What did the Egyptians do to the Israelites?   Exodus 1:10–14

7. How did the Hebrews experience the quality of life? Exodus 1:11–14

8. What solution did the Egyptian king plan for overpopulation? Exodus 1:15–22

9. How does the Catholic Church view this solution? CCC 2268

10. What are the implications of the fifth commandment? CCC 2269

11. Identify three heroines in Exodus 1–2 and explain their heroics.

* Identify a modern day heroine and describe her character.

12. What was the tribe of Moses' family? Exodus 2:1

13. Explain the drama in Exodus 2:1–10.

14. How do the New Testament Christians recall this event?

Acts 7:17–22	
Hebrews 11:23–26	

15. How was Moses educated? Acts 7:21–22

16. What happened in Exodus 2:11–14?

— How old was Moses at this time?   Acts 7:23–25

17. Where did Moses flee? Exodus 2:15

18. What did Moses do in Midian? Acts 7:29

19. Identify the members of Moses' family. Exodus 2:15–22

20. Describe what the Israelites were doing at this time. Exodus 2:23–25

* Choose a member of your family to pray for and bless this week.

CHAPTER 2

Moses in Midian
Exodus 3–4

God said to Moses, "I am who I am."
And he said, "Say this to the people of Israel, 'I am has sent me to you.'"
Exodus 3:14

A great amount of time transpires between chapters two and three of Exodus. Back in Egypt, one pharaoh dies and another takes the throne (Exodus 2:23). As many as sixty years pass, while Moses sojourns in Midian—he marries, starts his family, tends his father-in-law's flocks, sees the burning bush, and accepts the divine commission to return to Egypt. These are the hidden years of Moses' life.

Moses, who belongs to the priestly tribe of Levi, marries into the priestly family of Midian (Exodus 2:16). Therefore the marriage between Moses and Zipporah brings together the Hebrew and Midianite priestly lines. The compatibility of their priesthoods is demonstrated clearly later, when the priests of Israel share a sacrificial banquet with Moses' father-in-law (Exodus 18:12).

Moses was always a stranger, from his birth in Egypt to his death just within sight of the Promised Land. He was a refugee even in Midian, owning no flocks of his own. Moses spent most of his life as a refugee. The word for "sojourner" in Hebrew is *Ger*, and Moses chooses the related name *Gershom* for his firstborn son (Exodus 2:22). A similar name had already existed in Moses' family tree, because his grandfather's brother had been called Gershon (Exodus 6:16). Egypt was only a place of sojourn for the people of Israel, and now Moses is exiled even from Egypt.

"The bush was burning, yet it was not consumed" (Exodus 3:2). Moses knew the desert. He had grown up in the Nile Valley, where the desert is very near on both sides of the river along its whole long course through the African countryside. Except for the narrow strip of land irrigated by the river waters, everything in Moses' world was desert.

So Moses knew instantly when he spied the burning bush on Mount Horeb that something was very peculiar. The dry bush should have burned up in a flash but, instead, it kept burning on and on without being consumed. This was not a fire like the fires of this world. Moses knew he was looking at a miracle, something impossible by the laws of physics, and contrary to all his experience.

If the fire was not of this world, then it must have been of another world. Jesus refers to a similar other-worldly fire when He says, "I came to cast fire upon the earth, and would that it were already kindled" (Luke 12:49). This yearned-for fire is kindled when suddenly tongues of flame appear over the twelve apostles and the Virgin Mary in the Upper Room on Pentecost (Acts 2:3).

Since at Pentecost the Holy Spirit takes the form of tongues of flame, perhaps the fire in the burning bush is a revelation of the Third Person of the Blessed Trinity, the Holy Spirit. At the Baptism of the Lord in the Jordan River (Luke 3:22) and the Transfiguration of the Lord on Mount Tabor (Luke 9:35), the Father speaks from heaven, so perhaps at the burning bush the voice represents the First Person of the Blessed Trinity. If the voice is the Father and the fire is the Holy Spirit, where can one find the Son? Moses himself foreshadows Christ at prayer.

"What is his name?" (Exodus 3:13). From the burning bush, God gives Moses the knowledge of His Name. God reminds Moses that He never gave a gift so great to his forefathers Abraham, Isaac, or Jacob. Later, Moses learns the commandment "You shall not take the name of the LORD your God in vain; for the LORD will not hold him guiltless who takes his name in vain" (Exodus 20:7). Of course, one should never take anyone's name in vain, and so God will also give the commandment, "You shall not bear false witness against your neighbor" (Exodus 20:16).

God's name in Hebrew has four consonants *Y-H-W-H*. Scholarly writers call this by the Greek term *Tetragrammaton* (a word of four letters). When vowels are inserted, the word becomes *Yahweh* (or Jehovah), which means "He Who Is," or "He Causes to Be." Using the original meaning of the divine name, the biblical narrative reads: "HE WHO IS, the God of the Hebrews, has met with us, and now we pray you, let us go a three days' journey into the wilderness, that we may sacrifice to HIM WHO IS, our God" (Exodus 3:18). Again, "Then HE WHO IS said to him, Who has made man's mouth? Who makes him dumb, or deaf, or seeing, or blind? Is it not I, the I WHO AM?" (Exodus 4:11).

Jews avoided pronouncing this name altogether. Instead, as they read a text aloud they substituted *Ha-Shem* (The Name) or *Adonai* (Lord). Jesus and the apostles followed this practice themselves, as we find whenever the New Testament contains a quotation from the Old Testament. Every time medieval Jewish scribes copied the Name, they broke their pens, so that they could never be used to write a profane word. They knew exactly how many pens they needed to copy the Hebrew Bible.

"Oh, my Lord, I am not eloquent" (Exodus 4:10). As a youth, Moses was already bilingual, and as an adult he has to learn a third language. The Midianites were distant cousins of the Hebrews. Their father Midian had been a son of Abraham and half-brother of Isaac (Genesis 25:1–2). Hence the Midianite language was similar to Hebrew. The name Reuel is Midianite but could just as easily be Hebrew. The Hebrew Bible mentions four men of that name, three Hebrews (Genesis 36:4, Numbers 2:14, and 1 Chronicles 9:8), and one Midianite (Exodus 2:18). In either tongue, the name, Reuel means "Friend of God." Both languages belong to the Northwest Semite family, along with Aramaic, Chaldean, Syriac, Canaanite, Eblaite, Ugaritic, Phoenician, and Punic. Numerous inscriptions discovered in the Tentieth Century have made these languages and their relationships better known. Our knowledge of Hebrew has improved with better understanding of the cognate languages.

As Moses became fluent in his wife's language, he gradually got rusty in both Hebrew and Egyptian. When he arrived in Midian, the locals took him for an Egyptian, but on his return to Egypt, he would be taken for a Midianite. Moses objects several times to the commission to become God's spokesman. We should not assume that he had a speech defect. Perhaps, Moses simply knew he no longer commanded the high eloquence needed in a royal court, or the fluency of common speech to address the people. He may never have been as fluent in Hebrew as in Egyptian, because while in Egypt, the royal palace had been his domicile, while he visited his Hebrew relatives only occasionally.

At this early time, the arts of public address had not been developed. Only in the next millennium would the Greeks invent rhetoric and spread it throughout the world. There was still a low standard of general eloquence, and few people had the skills necessary to perform a mission like the one God asked of Moses. He was not uniquely challenged but simply unequipped for this extraordinary task. Fortunately, God did give those skills to his brother, so Aaron becomes spokesman for Moses, as Moses is spokesman for God. The Hebrew for spokesman is *Nebi*, or prophet. So Aaron will function as prophet for Moses, the prophet of God.

Moses took his wife and his sons and set them on an ass (Exodus 4:2). Back in chapter two we heard of Moses' firstborn son, Gershom (Exodus 2:22). Since then, a second son has been born, but remains unnamed. Later we will learn his name is Eliezer (Exodus 18:4), the same name that had once belonged to the faithful servant of Abraham (Genesis 15:2). One donkey is enough to convey the mother and two small boys for the journey back into Egypt. A larger family would need more than one donkey. The image of Moses walking along, staff in hand, leading the donkey with his wife and sons aboard, foreshadows a later time when Joseph escorts Mary and the infant Jesus into Egypt by the same route (Matthew 2:13–15).

Bringing the family down into Egypt, that place of slavery, must have been a difficult decision for Moses. He had a risky job to perform, and the safety of his family might be jeopardized in Egypt. Later, Moses will send his wife and sons back to Midian, to his father-in-law Jethro, who will care for them until after the Israelites have emerged from Egypt. The whole Exodus experience was not easy for Moses' family, as is often the case. Immigrants to America sometimes came as single men, went back to the home country to marry, returning without the wife or child until they could make enough money to send for them. Wives did not always like America, pining for their parents, and sometimes persuading the husbands to return to the homeland. Each immigrant family has its own story, as did Moses.

Zipporah and the boys slip down into Egypt with Moses and slip out of Egypt, leaving him there. Each time they traveled in or out of the country, they had to cross the Red Sea. Instead of donkey transport, the family would have to employ a *fellukah*, a combination sailboat and rowboat, using the sail when ferrying passengers in one direction and rowing with the oars to ferry them in the other.

"The Lord met him and sought to kill him" (Exodus 4:24). The narrative takes an unexpected turn when Moses, in the very act of obedience in returning to Egypt, encounters the harsh displeasure of the Lord. What is happening here? Why would God treat Moses this way? The next two verses reveal that Moses had failed to circumcise his son. God has asked him to do an extraordinary task, but Moses had as yet failed to do even an ordinary one.

One cannot pursue a vocation from the Lord without first making some progress in the practice of the basic virtues. How could Moses serve as leader for the whole Hebrew people, when he had not yet given his own son the sign of membership in that people? How could Moses negotiate a new covenant between the Lord and His people, when he had failed to follow the already standing Abrahamic covenant of circumcision? Abraham was inspirited by God to institute circumcision (Genesis 17:10), and Moses was inspired by God to confirm the practice (Exodus 12:28).

A time will come when circumcision will no longer be necessary for membership in the people of God, but that time was not yet for Moses. Even Saint Paul, the "apostle to the Gentiles" (Romans 11:13), praises circumcision as a sign of faithfulness (Romans 2:25), but the sign is not as great as the thing it signifies. So, in the New Covenant in Christ, the reality supercedes the sign.

"You are a bridegroom of blood to me" (Exodus 4:25). Zipporah performs a strange ritual, touching her husband with the severed foreskin of their son. She was not a Hebrew, and so her actions are more likely to represent the customs of her own people than of her husband's. The phrase "bridegroom of blood" occurs twice in the brief passage, and seems to provide a key to interpretation. Until this moment, Moses and Zipporah have been of different blood, one Hebrew and the other Midianite. Now Zipporah joins the people as well as the family of Moses. Zipporah uses an unfamiliar ritual to achieve conversion, but she is inspired with the same feelings as another foreign woman, who will join the people of Moses by the reciting the beautiful words:

> "Where you go I will go… your people will be my people,
> and your God my God"
> (Ruth 1:16)

When he *[Jesus]* talks about fire, he means in the first place his own Passion, which was a Passion of love and was therefore a fire; the new burning bush, which burns and is not consumed; a fire that is to be handed on. Jesus does not come to make us comfortable, rather he sets fire to the earth, he brings the great living fire of divine love, which is what the Holy Spirit is, a fire that burns.

Pope Benedict XVI (Cardinal Ratzinger), *God and the World*
(San Francisco, CA: Ignatius Press, 2002), p. 222.

---

1. What was Moses doing and what happened to him in Midian?   Exodus 3:1–3

2. In your own words, explain God's call on Moses.   Exodus 3:4–10

3. What did God reveal to Moses?

Exodus 3:5–6	
Luke 20:37–38	

4. How did Moses respond to God's call?

Exodus 3:6	
Exodus 3:11	
Exodus 3:13	
Exodus 4:1–3	
Exodus 4:10,13	
Exodus 4:20	

5. What does Moses learn in his dialogue with God? CCC 2575

6. What does Moses learn about God from the burning bush?

CCC 205	
CCC 206	
CCC 207	
CCC 208	

7. Who can approach the burning bush? CCC 2777

8. How can you know the name of God?

Exodus 3:13–15	
CCC 446	
Psalm 135:13	
Mark 14:61–62	

9. What is an appropriate response to hearing God's name? Philippians 2:9–11

10. How does God call people?

Exodus 3:4	
Isaiah 43:1–7	
John 1:37–39, 43	

11. Have you experienced God calling you? How did you *(will you)* respond?

12. What does God promise to those who follow Him? Matthew 11:28-30

13. Why is God concerned for His people?

Exodus 3:7–10	
CCC 1867	

14. What is God's objective? Exodus 3:10, 17

15. What does God command after the deliverance of His people? Exodus 3:12

16. Who predicts the king's response? Exodus 3:19–21, 4:21

17. Explain the signs that God gave to Moses.

Exodus 4:1–5	
Exodus 4:6–9	

18. With what emotion does God respond to Moses' reluctance? Exodus 4:10–17

19. What happened on Moses' return to Egypt? Exodus 4:18–26

20. Who did God send to meet Moses in the desert? Exodus 4:27–31

** Is God calling you to go alongside someone to help in ministry as Aaron did?

CHAPTER 3

Witness to Pharaoh
Exodus 5–6

**Thus says the LORD, the God of Israel,
"Let my people go!"**
Exodus 5:1

Encounters with the new pharaoh begin in chapter five. During his youth, Moses knew this pharaoh as his adoptive uncle, the brother of his foster mother. Once they had talked on a first-name basis. Now Moses has changed so much in appearance that the pharaoh does not seem to recognize him, and the change is not merely on the surface. Moses has lost much of his ability to speak, and perhaps even to understand Egyptian. Aaron serves as translator both ways. The conversations are reported to us as simple dialogues, but the actual exchange probably went something like this:

> Moses (in Hebrew): "Thus says the Lord, 'Let my people go.'"
> Aaron (in Egyptian): "Thus says the Lord, 'Let my people go.'"
> Pharaoh (in Egyptian): "Who is the Lord, that I should heed his voice?"
> Aaron (in Hebrew): "Who is the Lord, that I should heed his voice?"
> Moses (in Hebrew): "The God of the Hebrews has met with us."
> Aaron (in Egyptian): "The God of the Hebrews has met with us."
> Pharaoh (in Egyptian): "Get to your burdens."
> Aaron (in Hebrew): "Get to your burdens."

In this kind of bilingual conversation, the translator must remain as transparent as possible, yet the communication would be impossible without him. In our day, United Nations meetings and international conferences use the services of simultaneous translators who can begin reciting the translation even while the speech is still in progress. Some people are trained to translate simultaneously from English-to-Arabic, for example, while others have Arabic-to-English skills. Only a linguistic genius would be able to translate in both directions while speeches are in progress. Aaron translates both ways, but interrupts neither Pharaoh nor Moses, out of deference to their dignity as monarch and prophet of God. After each statement is concluded, Aaron translates it into the other language.

"I do not know the LORD" (Exodus 5:2). Pharaoh knew many gods, but he did not know the One True God. One of his predecessors, Akhenaten, had attempted to install the worship of one god, represented by the solar disc, Aten. The people's attachment to the old gods was too strong, however, and after Akenaten's death polytheism was restored in the country of Egypt.

In the time of Moses a new royal family installed itself in power as the Nineteenth Dynasty. Coming originally from the Delta area, not far from the land of Goshen where the Hebrews were concentrated, this family had a special devotion to the minor god Seti. According to Egyptian mythology, Seti had killed his brother Osiris in battle, sending him to the underworld to reign as lord there. Since he was guilty of the murder of his brother, Seti was not very popular among the Egyptians until the Pharaoh Seti I built a temple to him in Avaris.

The conflict between Moses and Pharaoh is not just personal, but also theological. The battle is between Seti, the god of Pharaoh, and HE WHO IS, the God of Moses. Pharaoh does not know the God of Moses, and Moses does not recognize the god of Pharaoh. The whole tug-of-wills over the release of the people of Israel must be seen in this theological context.

To Pharaoh, the Hebrews are slaves both in this life and in the next, so the God of the Hebrews is a slave god. The desire of the Hebrews for independence represents rebellion on earth but also in heaven. To Pharaoh, the God of Moses is an upstart, as the god Akhenaten was before him. The Moses' revolution comes on the heels of the failed Akhenaten revolution, and the Egyptian establishment does not want to hear about any changes whether social or religious. Pharaoh does not know the Lord and does not want to know anything about Him.

"You shall no longer give the people straw" (Exodus 5:7). Many of the tombs of Egypt have impressive wall-paintings that portray the activities of ordinary Egyptians going about their business—women mourn the dead, crush lilies to make perfume, and belly dance; men drive donkeys, train for war, and manufacture bricks. The laboring classes perform these duties for the pharaoh in this life, and in the after life they are seen as continuing to perform these same duties for the deceased pharaoh. So the Hebrews have been consigned to brick-building both in this life and in the next. By pharaoh's decree they stand condemned to eternal slavery. When they leave earthly service, they go to service in the realm of death.

The Egyptian grain harvest produced a large quantity of straw each year, and this by-product was used as bedding for the cattle, a low-protein dietary supplement for the livestock, roofing for homes, and material for brick building. Clay and water are the basic ingredients in brick manufacture, but adding straw makes the brick stronger for construction.

The Egyptians considered the Nile River and its agriculture to be the blessing of the gods. The priests controlled the agricultural economy, and the distribution of straw at the end of the harvest was the work of the temples. When Moses and Aaron invoked the name of an alien god, Pharaoh felt that they no longer deserved to receive any blessings from the gods of Egypt. Hence the supply of straw was cut off to punish them for their religious nonconformity. Here is one of the earliest historical examples of economic retaliation against a religious minority.

To the Egyptians, the withdrawal of straw was meant to indicate the withdrawal of grace as well. When the Hebrews could no longer obtain their raw materials from the religious monopoly, they had to go out into the fields to glean pickings, the desperate resort of the homeless and destitute. Alternatively, they could go to their Egyptian neighbors and religious institutions and beg for straw, a fate more demeaning than slavery. Since the men and boys were busy making bricks, the women and girls had to go out in search of straw, a blow to the self-respect and integrity of the nation. The Hebrews are being served notice that they may lose a place in the afterlife altogether if they are dismissed from the king's service. For now they still have the chance to be brick makers forever, but if they are reduced to mere beggary, they will have no place in the social order of this life or the next.

"You have made us offensive in the sight of Pharaoh" (Exodus 5:21). The Hebrews hated being slaves, but they hated even more being beggars. The immediate effect of Moses' intervention was not freedom, but even more difficulty. Moses and Aaron were at first received as heroes, but their popularity rating now plummeted. Throughout Moses' ministry this phenomenon recurs. The Hebrews honor Moses one moment, revile him the next. For forty years Moses will be riding a roller-coaster of public favor and disfavor. Many religious founders encountered both support and opposition, but Moses is subject to such ups and downs from his own people.

In the Middle East, a leader holds his position because he produces results for his constituency. The manner of coming to power is almost irrelevant, whether through inheritance, wealth, or election. Remaining in power depends upon how much the lives of ordinary people improve as a result of his leadership. Moses promises the blessing of freedom, but the immediate impact is an even harsher slavery. Therefore, to the people of such a culture, Moses is failing the test of leadership. For the short term, he is a curse and not a blessing to his people. The Hebrews think that Moses has made both them and their God look bad. The people do not give up on Moses altogether, though. They consign Moses and Aaron to the judgment of God, and do not pass judgment for themselves. Moses consults God again to renegotiate his contract. Rather than withdraw the mandate, God expands its terms.

"I will take you for my people, and I will be your God" (Exodus 6:7). Here we have the formula of every divine covenant. God offered a series of covenants to Adam, Noah, Abraham (twice), and now Moses. God promises in every case to belong to a progressively more concentrated group of people. In the person of Adam there was a bond between God and the entire human race; in the person of Noah with only his offspring, the survivors of the deluge; in the person of Abraham with the many nations descended from him; in the person of Moses with the twelve tribes of the Hebrews. On Mount Sinai this covenant will be ratified and confirmed, but the covenant is first proposed and negotiated here, in the midst of the first despair experienced by Moses during the course of his Egyptian mission. Until now, God only promised liberation and nationhood for the Hebrews, but now He bestows election as the people properly His own. There was no Chosen People until this moment, when Moses is in despair and the people are reviling him. The people are too crushed to heed Moses, "because of their broken spirit and their cruel bondage."

Instead of proceeding directly to the miracles, which will break this logjam in the narrative flow, the author cuts away to a recitation of the genealogy of the oldest sons of Jacob. That may seem an odd solution to the current impasse, but we should trust the human and divine authors to known what they are doing. They want to find the solution, not just in external miracles, but in the fact of who we are, created by God. God's remedy is Moses himself, and not just his deeds.

"These are the heads of their father's houses" (Exodus 6:14). Here is not a full genealogy but the fragment of a much larger family tree. Jacob had twelve sons, but only the three eldest find their place in this genealogical list. Sons of the same mother, they are full brothers to each other. Leah was the first wife of Jacob, and therefore held authority in the home. The Leah tribes seem to have been especially close. The very fragmentary nature of the genealogy implies that the Leah tribes were the initial focus of the mission of Moses. Members of the other tribes may have dwelt in other parts of Egypt, or even in the desert in the vicinity of the Nile Valley, at this precise time.

As the genealogy progresses it comes to concentrate on Moses himself. One learns exactly how Moses belongs to the priestly tribe of Levi. Moses is the son of Amram, the son of Korath, the son of Levi. Am-ram means "great people;" just Ab-ram means "great father" or "father of many." The two names are related as prophecy and fulfillment. Abraham was promised that he would be the father of great nations, and Amram has a name which means that. Korath probably intended that very thing when he bestowed the name Amram on his firstborn son.

The covenant with Abraham is very much on the minds of the Hebrew people during their sojourn in Egypt. They are multiplying to fulfill not only the fundamental imperative to Adam, but also the specific promise to Abraham.

Finally, there might have been somebody else named Moses around, as for example the four pharaohs named Tut-Moses or the thirteen pharaohs named Ra-Moses. The narrator wants us to know exactly who Moses the Liberator is, and the Semitic way to do that is to recite the lineage. Only when this point is settled can the narrative continue. That is why the genealogy concludes:

> *These* are the Aaron and Moses to whom the LORD said: "Bring out the people of Israel from the land of Egypt by their hosts." It was *they* who spoke to Pharaoh king of Egypt about bringing out the people of Israel from Egypt, *this* Moses and *this* Aaron (Exodus 6:26–27, emphasis added).

1. How does Pharaoh respond to the request to worship the Lord? Exodus 5:2

2. In your own words, explain the difference between *knowing the Lord* and knowing *about* Him. Job 42:5 *Do you know the Lord?*

3. What did Moses and Aaron want to do? Exodus 5:3

4. Find a common theme in the following passages.

Exodus 5:6–13	
1 Kings 12:1–13	

5. Explain the behaviors and perceptions of these characters in Exodus 5:13–21

Taskmasters	
Israelite Foremen	
Pharaoh	

6. What did the Israelite foremen say to Moses and Aaron? Exodus 5:19–21

7. How did Moses respond? Exodus 5:22–23

8. How did the Lord answer Moses? Exodus 6:1

9. What common things did God do for Abraham, Isaac, Jacob, and Moses?

Exodus 6:3	
Exodus 6:4–5	

10. What special thing did God do for Moses only? Exodus 6:3; 3:6, 13–15

11. Why does God take a concern for His people here? Exodus 6:5

12. Find the promise that God makes in the passages below.

Exodus 6:6–7	
Leviticus 26:12	
Jeremiah 31:33	
Hosea 2:23	

13. What promise is fulfilled in the following passages?

Genesis 15:18	
Exodus 6:7–8	
Nehemiah 9:8	
Psalm 105:8–11	
Sirach 44:21–23	

14. How did the people respond when Moses relayed God's promise? Exodus 6:9

15. What does the Lord ask of Moses in Exodus 6:10–11?

16. How does Moses respond to the command of the Lord? Exodus 6:12

17. Does God relent or change His plan? Exodus 6:13

18. What is the purpose of the genealogy in Exodus 6:14–26?

19. What virtue does God expect of Moses and all people?

1 Samuel 15:22	
Jeremiah 7:23	

20. How could you know the Lord better and obey His voice?

Isaiah 26:9	
Psalm 63	

* What will you do this week to seek to **know** the Lord more intimately?

CHAPTER 4

Ten Plagues
Exodus 7–11
Leviticus 13–14

This is the finger of God.
Exodus 8:19

Moses tried persuasion with Pharaoh, but it did not work. Now he turns to miraculous signs to demonstrate the divine authority with which he has been entrusted. Back in chapter three, when God first called Moses on Mount Horeb, He promised to accompany the mission to Pharaoh with signs and wonders: "I will stretch out my hand and smite Egypt with all the wonders which I will do in it" (Exodus 3:20). On that occasion God gave Moses three powers:

(1) Moses casts down his staff and it turns into a serpent (Exodus 4:3).

(2) Moses' hand emerges leprous, but then later it is healed (Exodus 4:6).

(3) Moses is given the power to pour Nile water out and turn it into blood.

When Moses actually gets to the court of Pharaoh, the demonstration of power turns out to be different and far more impressive. Aaron rather than Moses is the one who casts down his rod. There is competition from the wizards of Egypt, who also turn their rods into snakes, but Aaron's rod consumes theirs. Neither Moses nor Aaron performs the sign of the leprous hand. Not just a pitcher of water but the entire Nile River turns into blood, and that is only the first of ten "signs and wonders" which later readers of the Bible will call "the ten plagues of Egypt."

Commentators point out that snake charming was performed in Egypt from an early period. By use of music, the charmer hypnotizes the snake so that it becomes stiff as a rod, and can be handled safely. The magicians in the narrative are performing a reverse of the familiar routine, turning what appear to be rods into serpents. Pharaoh does not seem to be impressed. He actually finds the whole episode to be offensive, because the cobra was the ancient symbol of Upper Egypt. When the land was united into a single kingdom in 2910 BC, the southern cobra and the northern vulture were combined in the pharaonic headdress. Aaron's miracle insulted the royal crown and hardened Pharaoh's heart.

"All the water that was in the Nile turned to blood" (Exodus 7:20). The magicians of Egypt could easily, by use of a chemical powder or red dust, make a jug of water seem to become blood "by their secret arts" (Exodus 7:22). In chapter four, Moses was told to pour Nile water onto the ground to make it into blood, but here Aaron strikes the Nile with his rod and turns the entire water system of Egypt to blood. Some speculate that the reddening of the Nile may be related to the annual flood, but that was not catastrophic. Others surmise that the polluting of the Nile may be related to geological activity. Perhaps, but, even so, such physical causalities do not exclude the operation of the divine.

The Nile was not just one river among many others. Without the waters flowing northwards from East Africa, Egypt would be the most barren of deserts. So Egyptians considered the Nile a sacred river, the gift of the gods. To them, this act of striking the river with a rod was practically sacrilegious. The fouling of the Nile was an attack on both the gods and the people of Egypt, so the king's attitude is hard to comprehend: "Pharaoh turned and went into his house, and he did not lay even this to heart" (Exodus 7:23). He seems to lack solicitude for the welfare of his people, for whom the poisoning of the water is disastrous, and even for his own personal well-being, since he habitually goes down to the riverbank every morning—probably to pray as well as to bathe.

Christians should note that this miracle seems to foreshadow those miracles when Jesus turns water into wine, and later wine into His Blood. The banqueters in Cana and the Upper Room knew the Moses story well, and saw a profound continuity between the liberating miracles of Moses and of Jesus. There is also a connection between the Books of Exodus and Revelation, which foretells that "a third of the sea became blood, a third of the living creatures in the sea died" (Revelation 8:9), and "a third of the waters became wormwood, and many men died of the water, because it was made bitter" (Revelation 8:11).

"I will plague all your country with frogs" (Exodus 8:2). Frogs are more common in Egypt than in the Holy Land. The annual flooding of the Nile provides a rich breeding ground for the little creatures, which are seen as life-giving in Egyptian mythology. The Hebrew Bible mentions them only in connection with the plague of Exodus (Exodus 8, Psalm 78:45, Psalm 105:30). Frogs make only a single appearance in the New Testament, where they symbolize demonic spirits (Revelation 16:13–14). The previous plague may have a causal connection to this one. If the waters of the Nile become rancid, amphibious life will seek refuge on shore, a recourse not available to fish and other creatures that can live only in water. Even now the magicians of Egypt compete with Moses to make yet more frogs. You would think they should want to make them disappear instead!

"There came gnats on man and beast" (Exodus 8:17). **"I will send swarms of flies"** (Exodus 8:21). The third and fourth plagues—possibly a single plague in two parts—are related to the first and second plagues. Cattle go into the water to escape from pestering gnats and flies. When the waters of the Nile are fouled, the cattle have to remain on the riverbanks, victimized mercilessly. The flying insects multiply and then attack the inhabited area, which is never more than a few miles on either side of the river. With the third plague, Moses and Aaron completely outclass the magicians of Egypt, who have never been able to do anything remotely like turning dust into gnats. They are now compelled to admit, that these signs and wonders, are worked, by "the finger of God" (Exodus 8:19).

"A very severe plague upon your cattle" (Exodus 9:3). The fifth plague again results from the previous plague. The multiplication of biting insects spreads disease through the animal kingdom, and produces an epidemic of animal diseases. The external symptoms seem to describe anthrax, an infectious and usually fatal disease of warm-blooded animals, especially cattle and sheep, caused by bacillus *anthracis*. It is transmissible to man, and can cause malignant ulcers affecting various organs.

"Boils breaking out in sores on man and beast" (Exodus 9:9). The sixth plague is simply the spread of animal anthrax to the human population. All ten signs are called plagues, but only the sixth is a plague in the narrow definition: a highly infectious, usually fatal epidemic disease. Modern scientists have harvested strains of anthrax and combined it with delivery systems as biological warfare aimed at urban centers. On occasion, disease has been used as a weapon, when contaminated blankets have been hurled over city walls or distributed to defeated populations. Needless to say, wanton infection is a two-edged sword that can turn against the people who wield it. The common good requires the entire human race to stand together against epidemiological threats to world health.

Leprosy and plague have been terrible scourges down through history. When the Assyrians laid siege to the Judean fortress of Lachish in 701 BC, a plague broke out: "And that night the angel of the Lord went forth, and slew a hundred and eighty-five thousand in the camp of the Assyrians; and when men arose early in the morning, behold, these were all dead bodies. Then Sennacherib king of Assyria departed, went home, and dwelt at Nineveh" (2 Kings 19:35–36). This divinely ordained plague was the sole reason that the southern Kingdom of Judah did not fall, but remained independent for another 114 years, until the invasion of the Babylonians. Corroboration for the biblical account comes from the Greek historian Herodotus, who writes that the Assyrians were defeated on the borders of Egypt when an onslaught of field mice chewed their leather equipment to pieces. As we now know, rodents are responsible for the spread of bubonic plague.

Chapters 13 and 14 of Leviticus set up triage procedures for dealing with leprosy and plague. The Aaronic priesthood is entrusted with the responsibility to quarantine infected individuals. The Mosaic law distinguishes between infectious and non-infectious lesions and provides an opportunity for those who have been quarantined to seek to reenter society when their symptoms disappear and they are no longer infectious. The instruction "Go and show yourselves to the priests" (Luke 17:14) foreshadows the Sacrament of Reconciliation, which reintegrates the repentant sinner into fellowship with God and communion with God's people.

The Mosaic system, with its attention to good general hygiene, probably made the Jewish population less prone to infectious disease than other peoples around them. As a result their death rate was lower. Perhaps for this reason, the Syrian leper Naaman comes to the Hebrew prophet Elisha to seek a cure (2 Kings 5:1–27).

The quarantined individual suffers the loss of human society, of dignity, and even of divine favor, in some theological systems. To those who see the misfortunes of this life as a sign of divine misfavor, the poor leper who goes about shouting "Unclean! Unclean!" (Leviticus 13:45) announces his doom in both this life and the next. Jesus of Nazareth vigorously opposes this interpretation of human suffering, and the Synoptic evangelists emphasize the special care Jesus gave to lepers. Matthew and Mark show that Jesus healed lepers in Galilee (Matthew 8:2, Mark 1:40), and ate in the home of Simon the leper in Bethany (Matthew 26:6, Mark 14:3). Luke recalls the Naaman miracle (Luke 4:27), and recounts how Jesus once healed ten lepers, only one of whom returned to give thanks (Luke 17:12).

"I will cause very heavy hail to fall" (Exodus 9:18). Hailstorms can do tremendous damage to field crops, which are entirely at the mercy of the elements. Even trees can be stripped of leaves and branches and can die from shock. Both wild and domestic animals can die in large hailstorms. People who fail to take cover can also be killed by these hailstorms.

The land of Goshen, dwelling place of the Hebrews, is protected from this plague, as it was from the second plague of the flies. Situated on the edge of the delta, Goshen probably had fewer flies in general than the marshland itself. As for hail, it can be very localized, as any farmer knows. One field will be obliterated, while the field next to it will remain unharmed.

"I will bring locusts into your country" (Exodus 10:4). The farmer's biggest fear, as harvest approaches, is that locusts will wipe out all the work he has done preparing the soil, planting the seed, removing the weeds, and protecting the field from the incursions of wild animals. In an agricultural economy like Egypt's, the result could be a year's famine as well.

Grasshopper swarms seem to recur cyclically in dry countries. They eat everything for a few years, lay their eggs, and then hatch out after the vegetation has replenished itself. So a number of bad years will follow a number of good years, as in the days of Joseph (Genesis 41ff).

Viral plagues lead to abandonment of land, which in turn seems to lead to locust plagues. Those interested in this link may wish to read David Keys' *Catastrophe: An Investigation of the Origins of Modern Civilization* (London: Century Books, 1999), especially pages 294–295. The author David Keys describes the global crises of the Sixth Century AD, which resemble some of the Exodus phenomena.

A series of locust swarms ravaged the Holy Land in the days of Joel the prophet: "What the cutting locust left, the swarming locust has eaten. What the swarming locust left, the hopping locust has eaten, and what the hopping locust left, the destroying locust has eaten" (Joel 1:4). Like the first two plagues (polluted water and frogs), the locusts rear their ugly heads again in the Book of Revelation: "Then ... came locusts on the earth, and they were given power like the power of scorpions of the earth. ... In appearance the locusts were like horses arrayed for battle" (Revelation 9:3, 7). Locust swarms are often so thick that they darken the sky. So, locusts may have been involved in the eighth and ninth plagues as well.

"**Darkness over the land of Egypt**" (Exodus 10:21). In Egyptian mythology, the daylight belongs to Ra, the sun god, while nighttime belongs to the god of death. For people who worship the sun, an eclipse is a frightening occurrence. On June 15, 763 BC, Assyrian astrologers recorded a solar eclipse, which established the correlation between Mesopotamian and Julian calendars. The Romans, who were superstitious, found significance in the fact that eclipses took place soon after the death of Emperor Augustus in AD 14 and the death of Emperor Nerva in AD 98.

The Psalmist seems to evoke an eclipse when he writes, "Even though I walk through the valley of the shadow of death, I fear no evil" (Psalm 23:4). The plague of darkness leads inexorably to the final plague, the death of the firstborn.

1. What was God's objective in bringing Israel out of Egypt? Exodus 7:1–5

2. How old were Moses and Aaron when they spoke to Pharaoh? Exodus 7:7

3. What did God foretell about Pharaoh? Exodus 7:3–4

4. In your own words, explain the drama in Exodus 7:8–13.

5. Make a chart of the Ten Plagues of Egypt.

1)	Exodus 7:14–24	
2)	Exodus 7:25–8:11	
3)	Exodus 8:12–19	
4)	Exodus 8:20–28	
5)	Exodus 9:1–7	
6)	Exodus 9:8–12	
7)	Exodus 9:13–35	
8)	Exodus 10:1–20	
9)	Exodus 10:21–29	
10)	Exodus 11:1–9	

6. What was Pharaoh's disposition? Exodus 7:13

7. Relay God's messages in Exodus 7:15–19.

8. How did Pharaoh respond to the first plague? Exodus 7:22–23

9. What message did Pharaoh receive before the second plague? Exodus 7:25–8:1

10. How did Pharaoh respond to the plague of the frogs? Exodus 8:4–15

11. To whom did the magicians attribute the plagues? Exodus 8:15–19

12. What did Moses explain to Pharaoh in Exodus 8:21–32?

13. What did God explain to Pharaoh in Exodus 9:13–21?

14. Describe Pharaoh's response in Exodus 9:27–30.

15. Explain the three things necessary for true repentance.

CCC 1451	*Contrition*	
CCC 1455 CCC 1456		
CCC 1459		

16. What was God showing to Pharaoh? Romans 9:14–18

17. What does the Psalmist recall in Psalm 78:40–52?

18. List the events recorded in Psalm 105:26–36.

Psalm 105:26–27	
Psalm 105:28	
Psalm 105:29	
Psalm 105:30	
Psalm 105:31	
Psalm 105:32–33	
Psalm 105:34–35	
Psalm 105:36	

19. Pharaoh had how many opportunities to repent, as recorded in Exodus 7–11?

20. Catholics have the opportunity to taste God's mercy in the Sacrament of Reconciliation. When was the last time you availed yourself of this opportunity? Go to Confession at least once a season—fall, winter, etc., or more often if you can.

Monthly Social Activity

This month, your small group will meet for coffee, tea, or a simple breakfast, lunch, or dessert in someone's home. Pray for this social event and for the host or hostess. Try, if at all possible, to attend.

After a short prayer and some time for small talk, write one sentence about a "desert experience" you had. Then write another sentence about how God brought you through it. Try to share about this experience in a five-minute time frame.

Examples:

◆ *I had a difficult time figuring out what to do with my life when I finished school. God sent a counselor into my life who showed me a perfect plan for me.*

◆ *There was a period of unemployment in my family for many months. Ultimately, we were able to find work and stability.*

◆ *Early retirement seemed like a great idea. But, after a few months, I found myself getting more and more depressed. God provided an opportunity for me to serve at Church, which brought new joy into my life.*

CHAPTER 5

Passover
Exodus 11–15

**I will sing unto the LORD, for he has triumphed gloriously;
the horse and rider he has thrown into the sea.
The LORD is my strength and my song,
and he has become my salvation;
this is my God, and I will praise him, my father's God, and I will exalt him.**
Exodus 15:1–2

The miracles of God use economy of means. On occasion God suspends the laws of nature, but more often He uses earthly phenomena to achieve His ends. In the course of the first nine plagues, all means are clearly natural—water, frogs, flies, gnats, disease, hail, grasshoppers, and darkness. The instrumentality of the tenth plague is invisible, but nothing is subtracted from God's majesty if He employs some mysterious agent of nature. Later the seven sacraments of the Church will also use the matter of this world—water, oil, bread, wine, and words—to be transformed into divine presence and grace by the power of God. The natural aspect is so important that there can be no sacramental Baptism without real water, no Confirmation without real oil, no Holy Eucharist without first having real bread and wine. The reality of the natural matter becomes the springboard for a new reality of supernatural grace.

"All the first-born in the land of Egypt shall die" (Exodus 11:5). Some of those who want to find a natural basis for this plague propose poisonous gases as their theory. When volcanoes like Vesuvius erupt, most of the victims die from exposure to lethal fumes. For example, Pliny the Elder landed on the coast to pick up survivors, breathed the foul air, and died instantly. These gases are heavier than air, so they travel fatally along the ground rather than rising to a safe height. The typical Egyptian home had only a single entrance, and the father of the family slept in the vestibule, guarding the women and children within. During the warmer months, people used to sleep on the rooftop and take advantage of the cooling breezes. The firstborn son had the privilege of sleeping on a mat at the foot of his father's bed, right at ground level, while his younger siblings slept on the roof. Therefore, lethal gases at ground level would kill the firstborn, but spare the younger children. Attractive as this theory may be, the fact is that there are no volcanoes in the immediate vicinity.

"This month shall be for you the beginning of months" (Exodus 12:2). In the old Hebrew calendar in use before the fall of Jerusalem (580 BC), the New Year was in the spring, and the first month of the year (corresponding to March/April) was called *Abib*. The time of year when the flight from Egypt occurred is indicated in the description of the seventh plague, the hail: "The flax and barley were ruined, for the barley was in the ear and the flax was in the bud. But the wheat and the spelt were not ruined, for they are late in coming up" (Exodus 9:31–32). These verses describe the sequence of the harvest in Egypt and the surrounding countries. The earliest crop is flax in March, next barley in April, then wheat in May, and finally, the spelt in June. The first Passover took place while the flax was fully mature, while the barley was still budding out—precisely in early spring. Later, while they were in exile in Babylon, the Jews adopted a different calendar. First, they adopted the Babylonian names for the months, so the first month of spring came to be *Nisan*, rather than *Abib*. Secondly, in reaction against the Babylonian New Year, which was a major, eleven-day pagan ritual, the Jews shifted their New Year to the fall. So, the Jewish feast of Rosh-Hashanah, the "Head of the Year," is in the fall (September/October), rather than the spring now.

"You shall take it from the sheep or from the goats" (Exodus 12:5). In the ninth plague, when darkness was upon the land, Pharaoh agreed to let the Hebrews go, but he would not let the flocks and herds. What was Pharaoh's reason for not wanting to the let the cattle go? First, it is one thing for the hired hands to run off, but another thing for them to take the livestock with them. To pastoral people like the Hebrews and to agricultural people like the Egyptians, livestock mean livelihood and life. Second, the Egyptians actually worshipped their cows, though they were not as significant as in the Hindu pantheon; the Hebrews were not just asking to go, but to take some of the Egyptians' gods along as slaves. So, the death of the firstborn, the tenth plague, was all about the "sacred cows." The sacred writer takes care to reveal that the first-born of the cattle also died (Exodus 11:4–5).

At the Last Judgment, Jesus will separate the sheep from the goats: "When the Son of man comes in his glory, and all his angels with him, then he will sit on his glorious throne. Before him will be gathered all the nations, and he will separate them one from another as a shepherd separates the sheep from the goats" (Matthew 25:31–32). Christians may be surprised to learn that, in the Mosaic law, goats are just as kosher as sheep. "These are the animals you may eat: the ox, the sheep, the goat." (Deuteronomy 14:4). The very Passover lamb itself could be selected from either the sheep or the goats. The Jews listening to Jesus may have thought, "What a shame that all those nice goats are lost." The goats are lost not because they are by nature unclean, but because they make themselves unclean.

"When I see the blood, I will pass over you" (Exodus 12:13). The blood of the lamb is the redemption of the people of Israel, so they are spared the angel of death. Hyssop branches were used to sprinkle the blood upon the lintels of the doorways of the Israelites (the lintel is a cross-beam and the posts on either side of the entry). Ultimately, the blood of Christ becomes the blood of the Passover, so that all who are washed in the blood of the Lamb will be freed from eternal death. "These are they who have come out of the great tribulation; they have washed their robes and made them white in the blood of the Lamb" (Revelation 7:14). Blood is the symbol of life, and therefore, the perfect foil to the scourge of death.

The first Passover is eaten in haste, "your loins girded, your sandals on your feet, and your staff in hand" (Exodus 12:11). For this reason, the bread had no time to rise, and so unleavened bread becomes the bread of the Passover octave, a period from Passover itself to the eighth day following. This Passover bread, called mazzo, becomes the Eucharistic bread of the Roman tradition. The Eastern church, on the other hand, uses leavened bread for communion, varying from the Jewish custom.

"On the fourteenth day of the month at evening" (Exodus 12:18). The Egyptians used a solar calendar, as befitting their worship of Ra, the sun-god, but the Hebrews used a lunar calendar, because they originally came from Mesopotamia. Now in the lunar month of 29.5 days, the fourteenth day of the month is the exact midpoint, when the moon is full. So as the angel of death passes over the homes of the Hebrews, and strikes the homes of the Egyptians at midnight, the full orb of the moon is hovering overhead as a symbol of death. The Jewish Passover ceremony is, in a theological as well as a psychological sense, the antidote to the crazy, full moon. Easter always occurs shortly after Passover, on the first Sunday after the first full moon after the vernal equinox. When the Easter Vigil is celebrated outdoors in rural areas in the absence of artificial lights, the full moon overhead forms an awe-inspiring counterpart to the Easter fire and candle and tapers held by the congregants. Then the words of the Easter Exsultet take on deeper meaning: "Accept this candle. ... Let it mingle with the lights of heaven and continue bravely burning to dispel the darkness of this night."

"You shall tell your son on that day" (Exodus 13:8). Previously, Moses told the people, "And when your children say to you, 'What do you mean by this service?' you shall say, 'It is the sacrifice of the LORD's Passover'" (Exodus 12:26). During the Seder meal, the first meal of the Passover octave, the youngest adult male asks the father of the family a series of four questions:

* Why does this night differ from all other nights? For on all other nights we eat either leavened or unleavened bread; why on this night only unleavened bread?
* On all other nights we eat all kinds of herbs; why on this night only bitter herbs?
* On all other nights we need not dip our herbs even once; why on this night must we dip them twice?
* On all other nights we eat either sitting up or reclining; why on this night do we all recline?

Unlike Christian catechisms where one with more knowledge interrogates those with less, in Jewish tradition those who do not know asks one who does. Similarly, during the Last Supper narrative in the Gospel of John, several of the apostles pose questions to Jesus, knowing that He possesses all knowledge.

"And Moses took the bones of Joseph with him" (Exodus 13:19). The last two verses of the Book of Genesis describe the death of Joseph in the land of Egypt. "Then Joseph took an oath of the sons of Israel, saying, 'God will visit you, and you shall carry up my bones from here.' So Joseph died, being a hundred and ten years old; and they embalmed him, and he was put in a coffin in Egypt" (Genesis 50:25–26). Moses takes care to satisfy Joseph's dying wish to be taken for burial to the city of Hebron, to the cave of Machpelah, the tomb of his father Jacob, his grandfather Isaac, and his great-grandfather Abraham. For forty years the Hebrews will carry the bones of Joseph with them in their desert wanderings, until they finally enter the Promised Land and are able to lay Joseph to rest with his fathers (Joshua 24:32). To this day, both Jews and Muslims revere the tomb of the patriarchs in Hebron, although the two groups seem unable to coexist peacefully.

"The pillar of fire by night" (Exodus 13:22) — The signs and wonders continue to accompany the Hebrews on their journey. The pillar of cloud could have been a dust funnel kicked up by a prevailing easterly wind providing direction through the desert. The pillar of fire, however, is not so easily explained. Christian commentators have seen the pillar of fire as a foreshadowing of the light of Christ, as the Easter Exsultet proclaims: "Accept this Easter candle, a flame divided but undimmed, a pillar of fire that glows to the honor of God."

"He took six hundred picked chariots" (Exodus 14:7). Horse and chariot formed part of the armed forces of Egypt since the time of the Hyksos invaders four hundred years before Exodus. For swift attack like this one, single-horse chariots would carry two men each—a driver and a warrior. The driver would be slight of build like racing jockeys, while the warrior would be robust, though not heavyweight. The purpose of the military maneuver against the Hebrews was to break up the refugee train, and to bring back as many of the people and livestock as possible. This Pharaoh was possessive, but not genocidal. Pharaoh himself does not charge at the head of his forces. Like any other general, he seeks out high ground from which his signal corps can send orders down to the commanders. So, Pharaoh occupies high ground on one side of the sea, and Moses on the other. From the two sides, they see the same tsunami, but one sees the greatest miracle, and the other sees the greatest military defeat of all.

"Israel went into the midst of the sea" (Exodus 14:22). Throughout the Bible, the sea is a symbol of chaos. In the very beginning, "the Spirit of God was moving over the face of the waters" (Genesis 1:2). In the end, the sea will pass away. "Then I saw a new heaven and a new earth; for the first heaven and the first earth had passed away, and the sea was no more" (Revelation 21:1). The passage through the Red Sea, the heart of Old Testament salvation history, becomes the paradigm for liberation for the Jews from the slavery of Egypt, and liberation for all peoples from the slavery of sin and separation from God. As the preface for Thanksgiving Day reads, "Once you chose a people and gave them a destiny, and when you brought them out of bondage to freedom, they carried with them the promise that all men would be blessed and all men could be free." The ultimate freedom, of course, is freedom from sin and death. Therefore, the crossing of the Red Sea foreshadows the passage of the Lord Jesus through death to life, and our passage from sin to life with Him.

The Israelites witnessed marvels; you also will witness marvels, greater and more splendid than those which accompanied them on their departure from Egypt. You did not see Pharaoh drowned with his armies, but you have seen the devil with his weapons overcome by the waters of baptism. The Israelites passed through the sea; you have passed from death to life. They were delivered from the Egyptians; you have been delivered from the powers of darkness. The Israelites were freed from slavery to a pagan people; you have been freed from the much greater slavery to sin. ...

In those days Christ was present to the Israelites as he followed them, but he is present to us in a much deeper sense. The Lord was with them because of the favor he showed to Moses; now he is with us not simply because of Moses but also because of your obedience. After Egypt they dwelt in desert places; after your departure you will dwell in heaven. Their great leader and commander was Moses; we have a new Moses, God himself, as our leader and commander.

Saint John Chrysostom (347–407 AD), *Catecheses* 3, 24–27.

1. What did the Lord foretell to Moses in Exodus 11?

2. Describe some of the details of the Passover of the Lord.

Exodus 12:1–6	
Exodus 12:7, 22	
Exodus 12:8	
Exodus 12:11	
Exodus 12:15	

3. In the biblical sense what does "memorial" mean in Exodus 12:14? CCC 1363

4. What can you learn about the Passover Lamb?

Exodus 12:23	
John 1:29, 35	
1 Corinthians 5:7	
1 Peter 1:18–19	
CCC 608	

5. During the last Passover Jesus celebrated with His apostles on earth, who asked questions, and what questions did they ask?

John 13:36		
John 14:5	*Thomas*	
John 14:8		
John 14:22		

* If you were celebrating Passover with Jesus, what question would you ask Him?

6. What question is asked in Passover celebrations to this day? Exodus 12:26

7. How is this question answered in Deuteronomy 6:20–25?

8. What happened in Exodus 12:29–30?

9. How did Pharaoh respond? Exodus 12:31–32

10. How did the Egyptian people respond to the Israelites? Exodus 12: 33–36

11. What did God command in Exodus 13:1–16?

12. Why did God choose a longer route of exit for the Israelites? Exodus 13:17

13. By what means did God lead the people?

Exodus 13:21–22	
Numbers 9:15–22	
Psalm 78:14	
Psalm 105:39	
Wisdom 10:15–17	

14. What did Pharaoh and the Egyptians do in Exodus 14:1–9?

15. Explain the following responses.

The Israelites	Exodus 14:10–12	
Moses	Exodus 14:13–14	
The Lord	Exodus 14:15–18	

16. Explain the drama from the following passages.

Exodus 14:19–20	
Exodus 14:21–22	
Exodus 14:23	
Exodus 14:24–25	
Exodus 14:26–29	
Exodus 14:30–31	

17. What else can you relate about this event?

Deuteronomy 11:1–4	
Psalm 78:51–54	
Psalm 106:8–12	
CCC 2810	

18. Write your favorite stanza from the Song of Moses. Exodus 15:1–18

19. Who else sang and danced after Moses? Write her song. Exodus 15:20–21

20. Find God's promise in the scenario in Exodus 15:22–26.

** How can you listen to the Lord?

CHAPTER 6

Food from Heaven
Exodus 16–19, Numbers 11

**Then the Lord said to Moses,
"Behold, I will rain bread from heaven for you;
and the people shall go out and gather a day's portion every day,
that I may prove them, whether they will walk in my law or not."**
Exodus 16:4

The Middle East is drier now than it was during antiquity. Garden spots existed in Afghanistan, Yemen, Tunisia, and other regions that are deep desert today. The Sinai Peninsula also was more hospitable to nomadic, pastoral people such as Midianites and Hebrews. It was no "land flowing with milk and honey," but had more resources back in those days. Lone individuals or small groups could forage through the Sinai in those days, but a large crowd could hardly have survived for even a few days. People have suggested various natural explanations for the survival of the Hebrew refugees as they wandered for forty years in the desert, but natural means alone could hardly have been sufficient. God may have used natural wonders in Egypt, but in the desert He uses wonders surpassing nature.

"What are we, that you murmur against us?" (Exodus 16:7). Moses makes it clear that he is not a miracle worker. God is the One who works miracles, not His saints or prophets. Moses is only human, so he asks a rhetorical question: "What are we?" The word order is different in the Hebrew. *Nahnu ma?* meaning "We are *what*?" places the interrogative word in a highly emphatic position at the end of the sentence, rather than in the ordinary place at the beginning. If Moses had asked, "We are *who*?" then the answer would be, "You are Moses and Aaron, the sons of Amram." Instead, Moses asks, "We are *what*?" The answer will define the genus and species to which Moses and Aaron belong, namely, that they are human beings without any supernatural powers of their own.

"When the Lord gives you in the evening flesh to eat and in the morning bread to the full, because the Lord has heard your murmurings which you murmur against him—what are we?" (Exodus 16:8). Here again, the original text reads "We are *what*?" As the Passover Hallel expresses so well, "Not to us, O Lord, not to us, but to thy name give glory" (Psalm 115:1). All observant Jews recite this verse during the Seder meal of Passover every year.

Influenced by Moses and the Psalmist, the apostles too have occasion to stress that they are only human, even while divine power is operative through them. "When Peter entered, Cornelius met him and fell down at his feet and worshiped him. But Peter lifted him up, saying, 'Stand up; I too am a man.'" (Acts 10:25–26). Peter could have phrased a question the way Moses did: "I am What? Only a man."

Later, after healing a crippled man at the city of Lystra in Asia Minor, Paul and Barnabas are acclaimed as gods. "Barnabas they called Zeüs, and Paul, because he was the chief speaker, they called Hermes. And the priest of Zeüs, whose temple was in front of the city, brought oxen and garlands to the gates and wanted to offer sacrifice with the people. But when the apostles Barnabas and Paul heard of it, they tore their garments and rushed out among the multitude, crying, 'Men, why are you doing this? We also are men, of like nature with you.'" (Acts 14:12–15).

In another place, Saint Paul offers a theological reflection on this phenomenon. "But we have this treasure in earthen vessels, to show that the transcendent power belongs to God and not to us. We are afflicted in every way, but not crushed; perplexed, but not driven to despair; persecuted, but not forsaken; struck down, but not destroyed; always carrying in the body the death of Jesus, so that the life of Jesus may also be manifested in our bodies. For while we live we are always being given up to death for Jesus' sake, so that the life of Jesus may be manifested in our mortal flesh (2 Corinthians 4:7–11).

If we have power in our own rights, then, miracles are merely magic. However, if power belongs to God, then we are all on the receiving end of grace, both those who give and those who receive. God showed signs and wonders both to Moses and to the whole people. Moses was merely the instrument of God, the pre-eminent prophet within and not outside the body of the people. That is why Moses asks "We are what?" and not "I am what?" He reminds the people that they are only human just as he is only human.

"In the evening quails came up" (Exodus 16:13). The Exodus narrative reports three miracles that enable the Hebrews to survive in the desert:

1) Quail fall from the sky in the evening. Only one verse in Exodus mentions the quail, but there is a fuller account in Numbers 11, which records a tragedy after the miracle, when a plague, perhaps gluttony, causes the people to die after eating.
2) Water comes forth from the rock in Exodus 17 and Numbers 20. Moses falters in faith as he strikes the rock twice, and as a result incurs the punishment of not being allowed to set foot personally in the Promised Land.
3) Manna appears on the ground at dawn, the only one of the three miracles that is not followed by a hardship. The Exodus narrative contains the most complete account of the manna.

"They said to one another, 'What is it?'" (Exodus 16:15). Although the Hebrews wander forty years in the wilderness, they enjoy one of the privileges of paradise, to be fed by God. "The wilderness becomes a fruitful field" (Isaiah 32:15). When they see miraculous food spread out upon the ground the people are so amazed that they ask one another *Ma-nna*, "What, please?" This wondering question becomes the name for the substance. *Anna* is the Hebrew word for "please." Nine times in the Old Testament, prayers go up to God with the appeal *Anna Adonai*, "Please, Lord!" (2 Kings 20:3; Nehemiah 1:11; Psalms 116:4, 16; Psalm118:25a/b; Isaiah 28:3; Daniel 9:4; and Jonah 4:2). The short form *–na* can be attached to the end of other words, usually imperative verbs, to make them polite. The Hebrew word for "return" is *Shub*, and for "please come back" one says *Shub-na* (Psalm 80:14). Another such word is the familiar *Hosanna*, which means "Save, please!" (Psalm 118:25). The people of Jerusalem cry out *Hosanna* to Jesus on Palm Sunday (Matthew 21:9 twice, Mark 11:9 twice, and John 12:13), and *Hosanna* appears twice in the Sanctus of the Mass: "Hosanna in the highest."

The highest concentration of "please" words, four times in a single verse, is found in the Passover Hallel: *Anna Adonai hoshia-nna, Anna Adonai hatsliha-nna* (Psalm 118:25). This verse beseeches God in staccato petitions: "Please — Lord — save — please — please — Lord — deliver — please." The stark simplicity of the Hebrew plea becomes ornate in the English translation: "Save us, we beseech thee, O LORD, O LORD, we beseech thee, give us success!" (Psalm 118:25).

The people's question *"ma-nna?"* is an anagram of Moses' earlier question *"Nahnu-ma?"* The question word *"ma,"* starts one sentence, and ends the other; the syllable *"na"* ends one, and begins the other. The question "Who are we?" acquires new meaning in light of the manna. While inexplicable in and of itself, the manna provides an answer to the identity of the people. They are no longer "No people" (1 Peter 2:10), but have become instead the people uniquely nourished by God. Just as the manna confers dignity upon the people of the Old Testament, so the Eucharist gives meaning and selfhood to the people of the New Testament. The question "Who are we?" gets answered again, as God feeds us in an even more sublime way: "This is the bread which comes down from heaven, that a man may eat of it and not die" (John 6:50).

"On the sixth day they gathered twice as much" (Exodus 16:22). The manna from heaven comprises not one, but four miracles:

1) Manna from heaven appears on the ground each dawn.
2) Twice as much manna appears on Friday as on the other days.
3) No manna appears on the Sabbath.
4) The Friday portion of manna lasts for days without spoiling. Whereas, those who gathered more manna than they needed on other days and left part of it overnight found that it became foul and infested with worms (Exodus 16:20).

Three of these four miracles occur to protect the sabbath rest—in fact, to institute the sabbath, for the people have not yet received the Third Commandment! Now for the first time in the pages of Scripture the idea of sabbath duty takes shape before their eyes. The Book of Genesis asserted the sanctity of the seventh day, on which God rested (Genesis 2:3), but now in the context of the manna the human obligation of sabbath rest comes into focus. The curse of Adam was to earn his bread by the sweat of his brow (Genesis 3:19). With the gift of manna, God lifts Adam's curse, in part. The People of God will still have to earn their daily bread, once they enter the land flowing with milk and honey, but during the sojourn in the desert they receive gratis a bread for which they do no work except for gathering it. On the sabbath, they refrain even from gathering, to show that this bread is outside Adam's curse. Note that the manna predates the giving of the law. God nourishes the people before giving them the obligations of the covenant. In this way, manna constitutes pure gift, not a reward for services rendered. Never was God outdone in generosity, nor was His kindness ever limited to our merits.

"Let an omer of it be kept" (Exodus 16:32). Manna stays fresh for only one day's consumption, with two exceptions—the one already noted, when the Friday manna lasts through Saturday, and also a unique quantity of manna preserved in a special jar "throughout your generations" (Exodus 16:32). How many generations would that be? Another text promises, "Know therefore that the LORD your God is God, the faithful God who keeps covenant and steadfast love with those who love him and keep his commandments, to a thousand generations" (Deuteronomy 7:9). Since manna in the desert prefigures the Eucharist, the reserved portion of manna in a sense prefigures the reserved Blessed Sacrament kept in the tabernacle. The gift of miraculous nourishment stands as a continuing sign of God's loving care.

"Write this as a memorial in a book" (Exodus 17:14). Moses comes across in Exodus as a man who could write, who received the command to write, and who did, in fact, write. The literacy of Moses makes sense in light of the fact that he received the best education in the land of Egypt. Scribes did the work of official writing, and only skilled craftsmen carved the monumental hieroglyphic characters on stone. Nonetheless, there was a cursive kind of writing called *hieratic*, and an even more popular kind called *demotic*. Of the three kinds of writing, the adopted grandson of Pharaoh would be most likely to have a command of *hieratic*.

Moses could speak three languages—Egyptian, Hebrew, and Midianite. In Moses' time, Midianite and Hebrew did not yet have fully developed writing systems. By process of elimination, one could infer that Moses wrote in a simplified version of Egyptian script. In 1905, Sir William Flinders Petrie discovered "Proto-Sinaitic inscriptions" at Serabit el-Khadem in the Sinai peninsula, dating from 1500 BC. Laborers at Egyptian copper mines made the earliest known attempts to adapt Egyptian hieroglyphics to the Semitic languages. Several such attempts were made until eventually the Phoenician writing system came into being, and gave rise to the Aramaic (Hebrew), Syriac, Greek, Latin, Arabic, and Cyrillic alphabets. In the days of Moses, this graphic evolution was at a very early stage, still close to its roots in the Egyptian ideograms. Put simply, Moses has to use Egyptian script to put into writing the Hebrew traditions. Joshua, without the advantage of formal education, remains unable to read what Moses has written, and so God tells Moses, "Write this as a memorial in a book and recite it in the ears of Joshua" (Exodus 17:14).

"Moses' father-in-law offered a burnt offering" (Exodus 18:12). Jethro appeared earlier in Exodus, but only now does he take on strong personal characteristics. Recall that it took a number of chapters to discover that Moses' parents were called Amram and Jochebed (Exodus 2:1; 6:20), that his sister was Miriam (Exodus 2:4; 15:20), and that his second son was named Eliezer (Exodus 4:20; 18:4). The Exodus narrative seems to postpone the naming of minor characters, for the purpose of keeping them in the background. Only now does the narrative reveal that the wife and sons of Moses returned to Jethro at some point, perhaps when the mission to Pharaoh kept taking one turn after another for the worse.

Now, Jethro steps into the forefront, to help his son-in-law delegate responsibilities to others in governance of the large band of people under his care. "So Moses gave heed to the voice of his father-in-law and did all that he had said" (Exodus 18:24). Jethro, as a priest of the line of Midian, has inherited the religion of Abraham, and as father-in-law of Moses has received the revelation of God's true name at the burning bush. Jethro is a true priest, though not a Levite. So Aaron and all the elders of Israel partake in a ritual meal with him. While the people survive from day to day on manna, a miraculous bread from heaven, "Aaron came with all the elders of Israel to eat bread with Moses' father-in-law before God" (Exodus 18:12). Both of these events, the manna in the camp and the bread at the sacrificial banquet, foreshadow the miraculous gift of the Eucharist.

1. How much time elapsed between the time when the Israelites left Egypt and they started to grumble in the desert? Exodus 12:2, 51; Exodus 16:1–3

2. Why did the people grumble and complain? Exodus 16:1–3

3. Who did the people complain against? Exodus 16:1–3, 7

* Has there been a time in your life when you grumbled and complained to God?

4. What did God provide for the people?

Exodus 16:4–15	
Psalm 78:23–29	
Psalm 105:40	
John 6:31–33	
1 Corinthians 10:1–5	

5. What was manna like and how was it used? Exodus 16:31, Numbers 11:7–9

6. Explain the regulations for collecting the manna. Exodus 16:16–30

7. How obedient were the people? Exodus 16:20, 27–28

8. What did God prescribe in Exodus 16:23?

9. Explain the provision God made for posterity.

Exodus 16:32–34	
Hebrews 9:1–4	

10. How long did the Israelites receive the manna? Exodus 16:35, Joshua 5:12

11. Where do manna and every other good gift come from? James 1:17

12. What could be better than free food?

John 6:49–50	
John 6:51	
John 6:53–54	
John 6:55–57	
John 6:58	

13. Explain the daily bread, which is the source of immortality. CCC 2837

14. What happened in the following passages?

Exodus 17:1–7	
Psalm 78:15–16; 105:41	
Wisdom 11:4–8	
Isaiah 48:21	

15. What did the water symbolize? CCC 694

16. Explain the events in the following passages.

Exodus 17:8–13	
Exodus 17:14–15	
Exodus 18:1–12	
Exodus 18:13–23	
Exodus 18:24–27	

17. Describe the events in these passages.

Exodus 19:1–6	
1 Peter 2:9–10	
Exodus 19:9–13	
Hebrews 12:18–24	

18. In what manner did God communicate with Moses?

Exodus 3:4–6	
Exodus 17:8–12	
CCC 2577	

19. Explain the events in the following passages.

Exodus 19:14–15	
Exodus 19:16–19	
Exodus 19:20–25	
Psalm 18:7–15	
Psalm 29:3–10	

20. What do you profess when you eat the bread of heaven? 1 Corinthians 11:26

** What one practical thing could you do to receive the Eucharist more worthily?

Chapter 7

Giving of the Torah
Exodus 20–23

**I am the Lord your God,
who brought you out of the land of Egypt, out of the land of bondage.
You shall have no other gods before me.**
Exodus 20:2–3

God Is Love, and everything He does, He does out of love. Love is His very nature and He is constant. God knows everything. He knows what will bring us peace and joy. God also knows what will bring us pain and discord. In His goodness, He chooses to share with us the principles for living that will bring happiness and contentment. Understanding God's unfathomable love provides a solid background for understanding the laws of God.

Laws enable human beings to live together in society. Each and every human population has its own proper laws. Laws differ from country to country, even from town to town, but the world has never seen a completely lawless nation. Some laws, of course, are better than others, and the Mosaic law stands head and shoulders above the other legal codes of antiquity, even of modern times.

The Hebrew word *Torah* means more than just law, however:
❋ In the narrowest sense, Torah is the law given to Moses on the holy mountain.
❋ In a broader sense, Torah refers to the five books of Moses, which form a compendium of the divine–and–human legislation of ancient Israel.
❋ In the widest of all possible senses, Torah means the divine instruction provided to Israel by means of God's revelation to Moses.

Torah comes from a verb for "instruction" or learning. To the ancient Hebrew, the Torah gives guidance in human affairs, the way a roadmap charts out a journey. A traveler who ignores the map ends up making wrong turns and fails to end up in the desired place at the end of his journey. Torah is "law" in the same sense that a roadmap is "law." The One who knows everything has shown us the way, and those who choose not to follow the Torah, do so at their own peril.

Teachers teach and students learn. In the Torah, God teaches and Israel learns. Eventually the whole world will be drawn into the classroom of the Torah, but each and every individual must be drawn into the lesson plan of God. When we hear the Ten Commandments, as well as the other biblical laws, we need to look within ourselves and critique our own attitudes and behaviors. The purpose of the Torah, then, is for us to make a good examination of conscience. Moses did so when he first heard the Torah, as did the Israelites, and we stand in the long line of penitents who receive training in morality and ethics from the Word of the Lord.

"I am the LORD your God, who brought you out of the land of Egypt, out of the house of bondage. You shall have no other gods before me" (Exodus 20:3–4). God reminds Moses and the Israelites of His great saving deeds before He gives them the first commandment of the Torah. Note that salvation came before legislation. God did not say: Follow these laws and then I will bring you out of Egypt. First He brought them into freedom; then He instructs them on how to exercise that freedom wisely. Slaves do not need a Torah, because they function under the whip. Only free people need instruction. Wise people heed instruction. No one breaks the commandments; they break *themselves* against them!

The first principle of freedom is to acknowledge the Liberator. God is the Author of our freedom. We must not accept the gift, then spurn the Giver. The Torah begins by stressing the importance of our relationship with Almighty God. In fact, the Torah comprises a clarification of the obligations that inhere because of our covenant relationship with God. In any covenant or treaty, each party undertakes certain obligations on behalf of the other. God discharged His promise by leading the Israelites out of Egypt; now the Israelites have incumbent upon them the duty of being faithful to their saving God.

For Israelites to worship any strange god would constitute a grave injustice, not only to the God who saved them, but also to themselves and to their children. Freed people never freely sell themselves back into slavery. The Israelites were enslaved to the false gods as well as to the government of Egypt. They had to work in the forced-labor levee, which was supervised by the Egyptian priesthood. An infinitely more powerful God set them free from slavery to false gods. Those who worship strange gods throw away their freedom again.

When Moses and the Israelites initially heard the first commandment, they examined their consciences. For several generations they had sojourned in a land that worshipped false gods, but during that time the Egyptians themselves had tried to adopt monotheism. This commandment is a vindication for that noble effort, and the basis for the foundation of monotheistic religions. Strange gods have no place in Judaism, Christianity, or Islam.

Anything or anyone can become the object of idol worship. People are not divine, so worship of any individual person—rock star, head of state, loved one—would be idolatry. Things of this world are not divine. So, we should not place anything—material goods, clothes, sports, hobbies, money, education, jobs, homes, or cars—at the forefront of our thoughts, or in the center of our hearts. We should not adore our possessions, nor covet those of others. The implications of the first commandment get fleshed out in the remaining nine.

"You shall not take the name of the LORD your God in vain" (Exodus 20:7). Moses has brought the Israelites to the place where God first spoke to him and revealed the Divine Name. Now God gives a commandment about the proper use of that Name—only in prayer, never in vain. Once again the gift precedes the law. First God gave knowledge of the Name, and only later did He spell out the proper circumstances for its use. May His Name be praised forever!

Every Egyptian pharaoh had three names—a *serekh* name, a birth name, and a coronation name. The earliest rulers used the serekh name, framed in a rectangular cartouche (box). Soon the pharaohs began also to use their birth and coronation names, which appeared side-by-side in rounded cartouches.

During the Nineteenth and Twentieth Dynasties, the period of the exodus and following, thirteen pharaohs shared the same birth name Ra–Moses or Ramesses. They were distinguishable from one another, however, by their throne names. Ramesses I had the throne name Menpehtire, Ramessis II the throne name Usermaatre Setepenre, Ramesses III the name Usermaatre Meryamun, and so forth.

The Egyptian notion that every name has its proper conditions for use seems to correspond to the concept of the second commandment. God has made His Name known to us for prayer and liturgy, not for profane use. Moses and the Israelites understood this better than many English speakers seem to do today.

"Remember the sabbath day, to keep it holy" (Exodus 20:8). All ancient religions have festival days, which appear in the course of the calendar year—the New Year festival in many of them, nowhere more important than in Mesopotamia. Such festivals take people out of their ordinary lives into a higher sphere. The unique contribution of the sabbath law is that it brings the holy down to the level of ordinary life. The Greeks and Romans had no concept of a week. The Babylonians had a week, but with no concept of resting on the seventh day. This idea appears for the first time with the Mosaic law. The Bible itself contains no mention of the sabbath in connection with the patriarchs Abraham, Isaac, Jacob, or Joseph.

Ostensibly, the sabbath is a duty Israel owes to God, but in actual practice the beneficiary is not God, but the people themselves. Through the sabbath God receives worship, while the worshippers receive refreshment, rest, and peace. Every sabbath is a new passage through the Red Sea from the world of work and toil, that place of slavery, into freedom, that place of rest.

"Honor your father and your mother" (Exodus 20:12). When Moses heard these words, his thoughts went in two directions at once, towards his biological family and also towards his adopted Pharaonic family. On the one hand, he remembered his birth parents Amram and Jochebed, by whose wisdom his life was saved. Moses also remembered his Hebrew ancestors Levi, Jacob, Isaac, and Abraham. On the other hand, he honored the princess who had rescued him from the Nile, and provided an adopted family for him. He remembered her parents and grandparents, who were like family to him, too. Though he had fled from his uncle the pharaoh, and later pressed his case with his cousin the next pharaoh, he never dishonored pharaoh as the rightful ruler of Egypt. The people of Israel, however, did not always honor their spiritual father Moses as they should have in the Pentateuch. In dishonoring Moses, they dishonored the God who sent him. So honor given to a parent is really honor given to God.

"You shall not kill" (Exodus 20:13). There is something about this commandment, unlike the preceding commandments, which immediately looks for exceptions. What about war, capital punishment, or self-defense? Moses himself in examining his conscience recalls that once he killed an Egyptian. Of course, he did so to protect an innocent one. Nonetheless, the keen conscience of Moses must have troubled him for years.

This commandment itself is eloquently simple. Make what exceptions we may, the injunction to avoid murder stands in force. The very first actual sin, after the original sin of Adam and Eve, was the murder of Abel. The human race has continued to seek solutions to crisis situations by taking the lives of others. This commandment flies in the face of the culture of death. And instead of looking to excuse the exceptions, the human race would be better served by trying to implement the affirmation of human life that is contained within the rule itself.

"You shall not commit adultery" (Exodus 20:14). Again an eloquent simplicity stands over the elaborate rationalizations by which contemporary society operates. The marriage bond is a covenant like that between God and Israel, and to violate one covenant is to violate both. Through adultery a man and a woman place a false spouse ahead of their true one, and in so doing place a false god ahead of the True One. Idolatry and adultery occupy the same corner of the sinful soul, which says, "I will not be true." Unimaginable betrayal and misery result from this sin.

"You shall not steal" (Exodus 20:15). Tribal law generally forbids stealing within the tribe, while indulging theft from non–members. God's commandment allows no such double standard. We are not to take what belongs to our brother, fellow-citizen, stranger, or foreigner. If people and nations followed this commandment, there would be no war and no need for a wartime exemption from the commandment not to kill. Perhaps when Moses received this commandment he remembered how his ancestor Jacob had stolen his brother Esau's inheritance by tricking their father into giving him the blessing of the firstborn.

"You shall not bear false witness" (Exodus 20:16). False witness is a form of theft, stealing the reputation and rightful facts from our neighbor. False witness can constitute a form of judicial murder, when perjury happens during the course of a capital trial. Sworn testimony calls down heaven, and false testimony takes the name of heaven in vain. When there is no love for truth six days of the week, how could the sabbath be holy? Since God is truth, falsehood of every kind is a form of idolatry, worshipping the lie. Relationships based on lies cannot endure.

"You shall not covet your neighbor's house; you shall not covet your neighbor's wife, or his manservant, or his maidservant" (Exodus 20:17). The ninth and tenth commandments have to do with the interiority of the soul. These commandments save the Decalogue from commanding merely the outward observance of behavior, but ensure that the soul too must be faithful to the covenant.

Several of the commandments mention slavery. The first commandment recalls that the Lord brought Israel our of Egypt, "out of the house of bondage." The third commandment orders that male and female slaves shall rest along with their masters on the sabbath day. The tenth commandment orders that people should not covet the slaves of others. While falling short of banning slavery altogether, the effect of these commandments is to mitigate the practice of slavery among the Israelites, making it a very different thing from slavery in other cultures.

Slavery was much on the mind of the Israelites, for they were just emerging from a period of bondage as a people. Some of the Israelites themselves owned slaves, and brought them out of Egypt with them. There is a temptation to look back and judge them for not abolishing the practice of slavery altogether.

Following the Decalogue is a collection of laws about slavery, murder, and other topics. These seem to present some practical applications for the teachings of the Ten Commandments as related to daily life. Some laws are obviously a development along the same lines as the Decalogue: "Whoever strikes his father or mother shall be put to death" (Exodus 21:15). Other laws attempt to reconcile the high ethical standards of the Ten Commandments with the harsh reality of slavery: "When a man strikes his slave, male or female, with a rod and the slave dies under his hand, he shall be punished" (Exodus 21:20). Later, in Deuteronomy, the Ten Commandments will appear in a more abolitionist light. Apparently, the Israelites attempted to continue the practice of slavery, but the discrepancy with their own experience of liberation prompted them to begin the process of turning away from slavery, a process that finally bore fruit only in modern times.

The Ten Commandments planted a seed, and the ethical shade from that tree is still growing to give increased refreshment to the human race. The Torah gave birth to the Gospel, and we are still learning from the divine teaching contained in both of them. The perfect fulfillment of the law is seen in the life of Jesus Christ. "Think not that I have come to abolish the law and the prophets; I have come not to abolish them but to fulfill them. For truly, I say to you, till heaven and earth pass away, not an iota, not a dot, will pass from the law until all is accomplished. Whoever then relaxes one of the least of these commandments and teaches men so, shall be called least in the kingdom of heaven; but he who does them and teaches them shall be called great in the kingdom of heaven" (Matthew 5:17–19).

When a parent tells a child not to play in the street, or not to eat the delicious-looking berry that he knows is poisonous, he does so out of love for the child. The child might think the parent is harsh, but later will understand that the restriction was given out of love. God, our loving Father, gave Ten Commandments out of profound love for us. Let us obey the commandments and teach them to others.

> Moral obligation constitutes man's dignity, and he does not become more free if he discards it; on the contrary he takes a step backward. ... If there is no longer any obligation to which he can and must respond in freedom, then there is no longer any realm of freedom at all. The recognition of morality is the real substance of human dignity; but one cannot recognize this without simultaneously experiencing it as an obligation of freedom. Morality is not man's prison, but rather the divine element in him. ... The morality that the Church teaches is not some special burden for Christians; it is the defense of man against the attempt to abolish him. If morality—as we have seen—is not the enslavement of man but his liberation, then the Christian faith is the advance post of human freedom.
>
> Pope Benedict XVI, quoted in Brian McNeil, *A Turning Point for Europe*
> (San Francisco, CA, Ignatius Press, 1994), pp. 36–29.

1. List the Ten Commandments and a "sin" against each one. Exodus 20:1–17

I		
II		
III		
IV		
V *Exodus 20:13*	*You shall not kill.*	*Abortion*
VI		
VII *Exodus 20:15*	*You shall not steal.*	
VIII	*You shall not bear false witness.*	*Lying, Gossip*
IX		
X		

2. Explain the term "Decalogue." CCC 2056

3. Which commandment has a promise attached to it? Exodus 20:12

4. How did the people respond to the manifestation of God? Exodus 20:18–24

5. Explain the basis of the Ten Commandments and their full meaning. CCC 2061

6. Describe a person who claimed to obey the commandments. Matthew 19:16–26

7. Explain one of the laws concerning slaves. Exodus 21:1–11

8. List some offenses deserving the death penalty in this law. Exodus 21:12ff

Exodus 21:15, 17	
Exodus 21:16	
Exodus 21:29	
Exodus 22:17 (NAB) Exodus 22:18 (RSVCE)	
Exodus 22:18 (NAB) Exodus 22:19 (RSVCE)	

9. Define proportionality of justice as found in the talonic law? Exodus 21:23–25

— How does Jesus expound on *lex talionis* "the law of the claw"? Matthew 5:38ff

10. What can you learn from the following passages?

Exodus 21:32	
Matthew 26:14–15	

11. Explain some laws relating to thieves. Exodus 22:1–12

12. What should a man do after seducing a virgin? Exodus 22:15–17

13. How does God feel about widows and orphans? Exodus 22:20–24

14. How should a lender behave? Exodus 22:24–27

* "You shall not revile God, nor curse his anointed" (Exodus 22:28 [22:27 NAB]). How does this command impact the way you speak about your parish priest, your bishop, your leaders of government?

15. Explain the admonition in Exodus 23:1–3, 6–9.

16. Which commandments are reflected in Exodus 23:12–13?

17. What does God promise in Exodus 23:20–21?

18. What must you do to obey God? Exodus 23:20–22

19. Identify some rewards of fidelity to God. Exodus 23:21–33

20. Using the Ten Commandments, make an Examination of Conscience to use prior to Confession. Or, find a good Examination of Conscience and insert it here. Commit to making a good sacramental Confession this month.

CHAPTER 8

Pilgrimage to the Mountain
Exodus 24–30

**Now the appearance of the glory of the LORD was like a devouring fire
on the top of the mountain in the sight of the people of Israel.
And Moses entered the cloud, and went up on the mountain.
And Moses was on the mountain forty days and forty nights.**
Exodus 24:17–18

Moses Goes Up the Mountain. Moses spends forty days and forty nights on the holy mountain, and the Israelites will spend forty years wandering through the desert on their way to the Promised Land. In later centuries, the holy mountain will become a place of pilgrimage for Jews and Christians alike, as they seek to identify with the religious experience of Moses and the Israelites at this place. Many people come away changed for life, after seeing the dramatic location where God forged the covenant with Moses.

During November of the year AD 383, the holy Spanish nun Egeria visited the Sinai as part of an extensive pilgrimage to the Holy Land. The surviving manuscript of her diary begins with an excellent description of the topography in her day:

> When we arrived there our guides, the holy men who were with us, said, "It is usual for the people who come here to say a prayer when first they catch sight of the Mount of God," and we did as they suggested. The Mount of God is perhaps four miles away from where we were, directly across the huge valley I have mentioned. (*Egeria's Travels,* translated by John Wilkinson [London: Warminster, Aris & Phillips, 1999], p. 107)

The Bedouin of the area call this valley the Wadi er Raha (Valley of Rest), and the mountain Jebel Musa (Mount of Moses), an impressive outcropping of serrated reddish rock. The valley is clearly large enough to accommodate a large encampment of people.

> The valley lies under the flank of the Mount of God, and it really is huge. From looking at it we guessed—and they told us—that it was maybe sixteen miles long and, they said, four miles wide, and we had to pass through this valley before we reached the mountain. This is the huge flat valley in which the children of Israel were waiting while holy Moses went up into the Mount of God. ... It was at the head of this very valley that holy Moses pastured the cattle of his father-in-law and God spoke to him twice from the burning bush. From here we were looking at the Mount of God; our first way took us up to it, since the best ascent is from the direction by which we were approaching, and then we would descend again to the head of the valley (where the Bush was), since that is the better way down. (Ibid., p. 107–108)

In Egeria's time, the monks seemed to have lived more as hermits in separate caves rather than together in a single community. In her time, when the Roman Empire still held sway over the area, the desert was a safer place than it would later become.

> Pretty early on Sunday, we set off with the presbyter and monks who lived there to climb each of the mountains. They are hard to climb. You do not go round and round them, spiralling up gently, but straight at each one as if you were going up a wall, and then straight down to the foot, till you reach the foot of the central mountain, Sinai itself. Here then, impelled by Christ our God and assisted by the prayers of the holy men who accompanied us, we made the great effort of the climb. It was quite impossible to ride up, but though I had to go on foot I was not conscious of the effort—in fact I hardly noticed it, because, by God's will, I was seeing my hopes come true. (Ibid., p. 109)

Sister Egeria, like so many pilgrims before and since, experiences the elation that accompanies the ascent to a holy mountain. In so doing, they relive the experience of Moses himself. Imagine his feelings, climbing from the people of Israel gathered on the plain below, up into the presence of God Almighty. Mount Sinai is the paradigm for many shrines and monasteries that are found on mountaintops—Mount Tabor in the Holy Land, Monte Cassino and Subiaco in Italy, Mont San Michel in France, Montserrat in Spain, Engelberg in Switzerland, Mount Angel in Oregon, and many others elsewhere.

> We arrived on the summit of Sinai, the Mount of God where the Law was given, and the place where God's glory came down on the day when the mountain was smoking. ... All there is on the actual summit of the central mountain is the church and the cave of holy Moses. No one lives there. (Ibid., p. 109)

The actual mountaintop is quite small and barely has room for the present church, which stands about ten yards from the site of the cave, which has a mosque built over it. Egyptian President Anwar Sadat, back in the late 1970's, proposed that Sinai should become a center for Christians, Moslems, and Jews to come together, since they all believe in the truth of the revelation to Moses which took place on this spot. Sadat's dream currently stands in tatters because of the work of terrorists who assassinated him.

> When the whole passage had been read to us from the Book of Moses (on the very spot!) we made the Offering in the usual way and received Communion. As we were coming out of church the presbyters of the place gave us "blessings," some fruits which grow on the mountain itself. (Ibid., p. 109–110)

Egeria describes a Sunday liturgy atop the holy mountain, apparently the place where hermits from the area gathered. The Book of Exodus seems to have formed part of the Liturgy of the Word, no doubt along with a reading from one of the Gospels. The gift of fruit at the end of the service was part of the ministry of hospitality extended to pilgrims, who could grow faint after their long exertion of climbing the mountain. The monks had no doubt learned through experience that the pilgrims would fare better with a little nourishment. Such fruits as the desert provides have to be eaten within a short time after they are picked, because they deteriorate rapidly in the low humidity and heat of the desert air. So, Egeria experienced two kinds of "manna" here—the Eucharist, and the desert fruits. Pilgrims suffer from hunger and thirst. The desert fruits would have satisfied her physical hunger. Far better is the Eucharist which nourished her eternal soul.

> From there we were able to see Egypt and Palestine, the Red Sea and the Parthenian Sea (the part that takes you to Alexandria), as well as the vast lands of the Saracens—all unbelievably far below us. All this was pointed out to us by the holy men. (Ibid., p. 110–111)

In the clear air of winter, when there is less mirage effect from the heat, the view from the holy mountain is particularly stunning. One may sometimes see the Gulf of Aqaba to the east of the Sinai Peninsula, as well as the mountains of Egypt, which stand to the west across the Red Sea. Two continents stretch out below, Africa to the west and Asia to the east. Moses, in his day, could see the land of bondage in one direction, and the land of freedom in the other. This vision belonged to Moses alone, however, since no one else had an invitation to ascend to the very top of the mountain.

> Now... we began the descent. We passed on to another mountain next to it which gives the church there its name "On Horeb." (Ibid., p. 111)

Scholars differ as to whether Mount Sinai and Mount Horeb are actually one and the same mountain. Saint Jerome maintains that they are one and the same. Eusebius and Egeria indicate that they are two different mountains. Clearly the area has a lot of mountains to choose from, and many places have more than one name. Egeria attends a second Sunday liturgy here, but does not mention that she received Holy Communion a second time.

> When we had made the Offering, we set off again, with the presbyters and monks pointing things out to us, to another place not far away. It is where Aaron and the seventy elders stood while holy Moses received from the Lord the Law for the children of Israel. There is no building there, but it is an enormous round rock with a flat place on top where the holy men are said to have stood, and a kind of altar in the middle made of stones. So there too we had a passage read from the Book of Moses and an appropriate psalm. (Ibid., p. 111–112)

Egeria does not mention which psalm she used as a response to the reading, but the Book of Psalms contains only eight references to the name of Moses, and three of these are to be found in Psalm 106, verses 16, 23, and 32. For this reason, one may surmise that Egeria and the others may have recited this historical psalm, which recounts the events of Exodus. Another possibility is Psalm 90, whose title proclaims itself to be "A prayer of Moses, the man of God."

Our way out took us to the head of this valley ... at the place of the Bush (which is still alive and sprouting). It was about four o'clock by the time we had come right down the Mount and reached the Bush. (Ibid., p. 112)

Within a century of Egeria's time, the monks will build the monastery of Saint Catherine at the site of the burning bush, with fortress-like walls to prevent the incursion of marauders. During the period of iconoclasm, when all the icons of the Byzantine world were destroyed, Saint Catherine's stood outside the territory of the iconoclastic emperors, and her icons were spared. Hence, some of the earliest Christian art is now to be seen at this Sinai monastery.

These monks have an important library. Here during the Nineteenth Century, the Russian traveler Von Tischendorf discovered one of the oldest copies of the Greek Bible, the Codex Sinaiticus, which found its way first to the Hermitage Museum in Saint Petersburg, Russia, and then on to the British Museum, where it remains.

Right at the head of the valley, where we had spent the night and seen the Burning Bush out of which God spoke to holy Moses, we saw also the place where Moses was standing before the Bush, when God said to him, "Undo the fastening of thy shoes: for the place whereon thou standest is holy ground." And now that we were leaving the Bush, they showed us the rest of the places. ... So we were shown everything which the Books of holy Moses tell us took place in that valley beneath holy Sinai, the Mount of God. (Ibid., p. 112–113)

The pilgrim differs from the tourist. Although both travel in the body, the pilgrim travels also in the spirit. The pilgrim strives to grow in grace, while the tourist accumulates photographs and souvenirs. As a result, the pilgrim comes home changed, while the tourist does not. The passage of tourists in large numbers through a country leaves behind litter and erosions, whereas pilgrims respect the local people. After the passage of pilgrims, a holy place may become even holier. Moses himself was never the same after his experience on the mountaintop, but the mountains also acquired new meaning. For this reason, Egeria could be profoundly moved by her experience at the same mountain.

I know that I should never cease to give thanks to God, but I thank him especially for this wonderful experience he has given me, beyond anything I could expect or deserve. I am far from worthy to have visited all these holy places. And I cannot do enough to express my gratitude to all the holy men who so kindly and willingly welcomed so unimportant a person as me [*sic*]. (Ibid., p. 114)

Egeria's translator, Reverend John Wilkinson of Saint George's College, gave a talk on "Jerusalem during the Byzantine period," in Jerusalem in 1975. He radiated enthusiasm for early Christian shrines and the patristic writings about them.

The course of history has not been kind to the holy places of antiquity, nor even to the unholy places. The falling and rising of civilizations have brought about the erosion of formerly habitable land, the extension of the desert, and the destruction of fragile landmarks and buildings. The Sinai desert today cannot sustain a population as large as the Sinai of Moses' or of Egeria's time. Nonetheless, the awesome topography still succeeds in communicating a sense of the dramatic experience that Moses and the Israelites shared, and the spirit of hospitality still extends itself to those intrepid pilgrims who attempt the ascent of the holy mountain. After such a visit, peace on earth seems almost tangible, just within our reach. For many pilgrims, the visit to Mount Sinai is the experience of a lifetime.

An American teenager, Deirdre McNamer of Billings, Montana, made the following diary entry right after she and her mother Elizabeth came down from the holy mountain:

> June 9, 1988 — I will never forget today. We got up at five in the morning and hiked two hours (in the dark) to the top of Mount Moses. From here we bought tea and biscuits from a bedouin, and watched the sun rise ... one of the most precious, beautiful things I have ever seen. Afterwards, we hiked back down. We had a tour of the monastery. Then (being the adventurers we are) we rode camels to the village.

1. Describe the scenario in Exodus 24:1–11.

2. What did God intend to give to Moses? Exodus 24:12

3. What happened when Moses went up the mountain? Exodus 24:15–18

4. What part of the Covenant fell to the people? CCC 2060

5. Which manifestation is common to these passages?

Exodus 24:15	
Luke 1:35	
Luke 9:34–35	
Luke 21:27	
Acts 1:9	

6. Explain the images above. CCC 697

7. Describe or draw the ark of the covenant. Exodus 25:1–22

8. What should always be kept on the table? Exodus 25:30

9. Describe the Tabernacle or "Dwelling." Exodus 26:1–37

Exodus 26:1–14	
Exodus 26:15–30	
Exodus 26:31–37	

10. Briefly describe the Altar of Holocausts. Exodus 27:1–8

11. What was the court of the tabernacle like? Exodus 27:9–19

12. Why would the Israelites need olive oil? Exodus 27:20–21

13. Briefly describe the priestly vestments.

Exodus 28:1–5	
Exodus 28:6–21	
Exodus 28:22–30	
Exodus 28:31–42	

14. Explain the ritual of ordination of priests. Exodus 29:1–46

15. Describe the altar of incense. Exodus 30:1–10

16. After a census, what must each Israelite do? Exodus 30:11–16

17. What would the priests use for washing? Exodus 30:17–21

18. Explain the uses of anointing oil. Exodus 30:22–33

19. What guidelines did the Lord give concerning incense? Exodus 30:34–38

20. Explain the "sense of the sacred" owed to God. CCC 2144

** Share a time when you went on a retreat or pilgrimage to hear the Lord.

Monthly Social Activity

This month, your small group will meet for coffee, tea, or a simple breakfast, lunch, or dessert in someone's home. Pray for this social event and for the host or hostess. Try, if at all possible, to attend.

After a short prayer and some time for small talk, write one sentence about a "pilgrimage experience" you had. Then write another sentence about the highlight of this time. Try to share about this experience in a five-minute time frame.

Examples:

◆ *I went to a nearby parish for a wedding, and was enthralled by the beauty of the church.*

◆ *On a trip to Washington DC to March for Life, I visited the National Basilica of the Immaculate Conception.*

◆ *When a close family member was diagnosed with a serious illness, we went on pilgrimage to Lourdes.*

CHAPTER 9

The Golden Calf
Exodus 31–34

**And he said, "I will make all my goodness pass before you,
and will proclaim before you my name 'The Lᴏʀᴅ';
and I will be gracious to whom I will be gracious,
and will show mercy on whom I will show mercy,
But," he said, "you cannot see my face;
for a man shall not see me and live."**
Exodus 33:19–20

The people of Israel wait patiently, then get impatient, and finally wait no longer. Forty days is a very long time for Moses, or any other leader, to be absent. Imagine a home where parents disappear for over a month. Imagine a classroom where the teacher leaves for six weeks.

Once a high-school teacher found his afternoon class restless. He invited the students to pretend that he was not there, and to do whatever they liked for sixty seconds. One young man got on top of his desk and hopped from desktop to desktop, as the rest of the students watched in a state of amazement along with their teacher. At the sixtieth second, the boy reached the last desk. If so much mayhem is possible in a single minute, how much could happen in the course of 28,800 minutes (forty days)?

Jesus spent forty days and forty nights in the desert, but that was before the call of the apostles. Had He retreated a year or two later, the momentum of His public ministry would have been broken. He frequently withdrew for prayer, but never for such a lengthy period of time.

During his own forty days of contemplation, Moses was not neglecting the people. Aaron and the seventy elders had been delegated to care for them. Moses himself had a lot of work to do, receiving instructions for them from the Lord. Whenever he wished he could look down and contemplate the great mass of the people, and he was probably not surprised when the Lord told him that they had been sinning.

"I have called by name Bezalel" (Exodus 31:1). Among the last of the instructions which Moses received while he was still on the mountain, was the appointment of the chief artisans to construct the tent of meeting and its furnishings—the ark of the covenant and the mercy seat, the table and lampstand, the altars of incense and of burnt offering, and all their utensils. God mentions the two chief artisans by name—Bezalel son of Uri, and Oholiab son of Ahis—who are to be joined by all able men. These men possess three important qualities, useful in the Lord's service:

(1) They come from two tribes other than the tribe of Levi. Bezalel comes from the tribe of Judah, and Oholiab from the tribe of Dan. So craftsmen from the eleven "lay" tribes receive the appointment to construct the sacred objects for use by Levi, the priestly tribe. In this way all the tribes come to participate in the liturgy of Israel. In many churches, families donate sacred objects for use at the altar, sometimes for decades or centuries. Every time a chalice donated by a particular family finds use in sacred liturgy, that family participates in the action of the altar.

(2) Bezalel, Oholiab, and all others with the requisite skills are to help in constructing the sacred objects. Every one of the tribes had members with some of the talents needed. They had learned and practiced these skills in Egypt. The Pharaohs used craftsmen of any nationality in working with precious metals, fashioning jewelry for their wives and daughters, and building fancy objects for their leisure use. When the archaeologist Howard Carter opened the only unpillaged pharaonic tomb in the Valley of the Kings, he revealed to the world the priceless playthings used in life by the boy-king Tutankhamun only a few decades before the Exodus. Hebrew craftsmen, perhaps even Bezalel and Oholiab in their youth, may have contributed to the construction of those pharaonic objects.

The pharaohs were not the only people in Egypt, however, who owned such things. Ernest Schiaparelli discovered the intact tomb of the official Khai at Der el-Medina in 1906, with an inlaid wooden chest and a 46-foot-long brightly painted papyrus scroll of the Book of the Dead. In the same excavations he found the tomb of the noted painter May with appropriately fine pieces in both plaster and painted bas-relief. All these items found a home in Turin, Italy, at the Museo Egizio, considered one of the finest collections of Egyptian antiquities in the world. Egypt had plenty of artisans, and they could make their own art, but anyone with the talent of Bezalel and Oholiab would have also been employed there.

(3) Bezalel is filled with the Spirit of God (Exodus 31:3). God insists that the artisan who works on the liturgical objects should be inspired with the grace of God. Still to this day, the Byzantine tradition requires that iconographers should be in a state of grace while they write sacred icons. (The correct verb for making an icon is "to write" not "to paint" because the icon describes a sacred subject.) When the artist is filled with God, the creation of art is a divine activity, like the creation of the world. Certainly one would not want to use a chalice on the altar if the craftsman had been cursing and swearing while fashioning it. The rite of blessing a chalice assumes that loving and faithful care has gone into the crafting of the piece.

"Make us gods, who shall go before us" (Exodus 32:1). Unfortunately some of the fine craftsmen, whom God wished to enlist in making objects for true worship, at that very moment, were finding employment in an ignoble task, the fashioning of the golden calf—an idol. The person who worships a false idol becomes like that dead god, but the one who worships the Living God becomes like Him.

Before Moses went up the mountain, he read to the people the Book of the Covenant, which he himself had written, and the Israelites agreed to follow these laws (Exodus 24:7). Some of the provisions of that covenant to which the Israelites did not remain faithful during Moses' absence follow:

* ❋ "You shall have no other gods before me" (Exodus 20:3).
* ❋ "You shall not make for yourself a graven image" (Exodus 20:4).
* ❋ "Whoever sacrifices to any god, save to the Lord only, shall be utterly destroyed" (Exodus 22:20).
* ❋ "You shall not revile God, nor curse a ruler of your people" (Exodus 22:28).
* ❋ "Three times in the year you shall keep a feast to me" (Exodus 23:14).

The cumulative effect of all these commandments was to forbid exactly the kind of behavior in which the Hebrews indulged during Moses' absence.

Idolatry is a fundamental sin, a violation of the very first commandment. Pride, foremost of the vices, prompts people to adore themselves, or something other than the One worthy of worship. Adam and Eve's original sin was far more than the eating of a forbidden fruit—they wished to become gods in place of the One, True God. Since that unhappy beginning, each and every actual sin has perpetuated the original rebellion. The liar rebels against the Truth of God, the murderer against the Life of God, the adulterer against the Faithfulness of God.

During their sojourn in Egypt, the Israelites were continually exposed to idolatry, and some fell into that sin. As a result, even after the great displays of divine power, even while Moses is meeting God on the mountaintop above them, they forge a false god to worship. Why did they fashion their idol from gold? Gold is a soft metal and their idol would not be very sturdy. Gold, of course, has been used as coinage from earliest times. The Poles still call their currency the *zloty* (gold-piece) and, until the recent coming of the Euro, the Dutch still called theirs the gilder.

When the Israelites made an idol of gold, they were worshipping money. In the pantheon of false gods, money holds a high place. No matter how much money some people get, they never feel they have enough. People are jealous of those who have more. The poor want to be rich, and the rich want to be richer. The preaching of Jesus in the Sermon on the Mount (Matthew chapters 5–7) debunks this false worship of money. The golden calf is the epitome of this false religion.

Why did they fashion an idol in the form of a calf? Back in Egypt one of the many false gods was Hathor, the cow goddess. The cow and the oxen are indigenous to river valleys like that of the Nile, and symbolize prosperity and abundance. For example, the Brahma bull represents the highest divinity in India. Also, the calf is a symbol of a new generation of life, and so something of a fertility symbol as well. Even the Israelites, who did not identify cattle with divinity, refused to leave Egypt without their cattle.

The Hebrews left Egypt and her gods behind, and when Moses was too slow to satisfy them, they started to turn back to the Egyptian gods again. This was like a second fall of Man, so God offered to kill them all and start a new people from Moses himself. Perhaps this was a test for Moses, just as the sacrifice of Isaac had been a test for Abraham. If so, Moses passes his test just as Abraham did. Both of them find a solution other than the annihilation of the people.

Aaron shows himself to be weak in character in this episode. Moses appointed him as his lieutenant both to lead in Moses' absence and to assist in his presence. That should have been enough for him. He does not attempt to seize power willfully, but he does allow the reigns of power to be thrust upon him, as Shakespeare's writes, "Some are born great, some achieve greatness and some have greatness thrust upon them" (*Twelfth Night,* Act Two, Scene 5). Leadership was thrust upon Aaron, but greatness was not the result.

The first High Priest in Israelite history, the founder of the Aaronic priesthood, builds a false god for the people to worship! The Levitical priesthood does not get off to a very good start here. The very first step is a detour. Later, in the time of the prophets and again in the time of Jesus, the high priests will fail to distinguish themselves with critical insight. The greatest descendant of Aaron will be John the Baptist, son of the priest Zachary and his wife Elizabeth, who is called a "daughter of Aaron." In the time of visitation, the descendents of Aaron will exonerate their ancestor's weakness and folly.

"Slay every man and his brother" (Exodus 32:27). Moses imposes a death sentence upon three thousand Hebrews in the aftermath of the golden calf incident. Sword-wielding Levitical priests wend their way through the camp, slaughtering their countrymen. Is this really the will of God, or just Moses' idea? The text does not say that God commanded it. Moses unfortunately initiates a streak of violence that will run throughout the Hebrew tradition.

Seeds of violence are planted between Levi and the rest of the tribes, and that violence will resurface in the time of the Judges and of King Saul, when the Benjaminites will slaughter Levites. Violence begets violence. There is a chain of violence, and the only way to stop the violence is to break the chain. The Gospel value of forgiveness is the only antidote to violent ways of history. The death penalty does not give any real closure, even when the sentence is just.

Pertinent to the golden calf incident is the commandment, "Whoever sacrifices to any god, save to the Lord only, shall be utterly destroyed" (Exodus 22:20). The Mosaic law seems to attach the death penalty to a number of crimes. The most common formula is the use of the concluding phrase *mot yumat,* which means "with death he shall die" or "surely he shall die." Seven times the Book of Exodus seemingly uses this phrase to legislate the death penalty:

Exodus 19:13 — For attempting to follow Moses up the mountain.
Exodus 21:12 — For beating a man to death.
Exodus 21:15 — For striking one's father or mother.
Exodus 21:16 — For abduction or kidnapping.
Exodus 21:17 — For cursing one's father or mother.
Exodus 22:19 — For bestiality.
Exodus 31:14 — For profaning the sabbath day.

Of course, the phrase "surely he shall die" is true of every man and woman ever born. All are subject to death. Death can be honorable or dishonorable. When Catholics pray for a happy death, we ask God to give grace at the moment of transition into the next life. At the end of every Hail Mary we ask the Blessed Virgin, "Pray for us sinners, now and at the hour of our death." Even Jesus Christ submitted to death—the ignominious death of the Cross. (Philippians 2:8)

What kind of a death penalty does the Mosaic law invoke—the death of the body or the death of the soul? If one man beats another to death he shall surely die (Exodus 21:12), whether or not he is executed. He dies the death of a murderer, even if he dies quietly in his own bed. From the time he takes a life and the time he gives up his own, he shall walk about the earth with a dead soul inside a living body. He committed a mortal sin, dealing a spiritual deathblow to his own soul, while dealing a physical deathblow to the body of another person. This crime has an "ipso-facto" death penalty attached to it. God proscribes that the sinner shall die, but not that he must be killed. The sinner kills himself by his own sin. God says, "I do not wish the sinner to die but to live," encouraging repentance.

Several times the Book of Revelation refers to "the second death" (Revelation 2:11, 20:6, 20:14 and 21:8). This phrase refers not to the death of the body, but to that "second death" of the soul, eternal damnation, unless he repents. We should, by avoiding idolatry of all kinds, ensure that while there is life in our bodies, our souls too shall remain alive. Then when the hour of the first death comes, we will be able to enter into eternal adoration of the Living God.

> Blessed and holy is he who shares in the first resurrection!
> Over such the second death has no power,
> but they shall be priests of God and of Christ,
> and they shall reign with him a thousand years.
> Revelation 20:6

1. Who chose the artisans for work? Exodus 31:1–11

2. Explain the sabbath laws. Exodus 31:12–17

3. What happened when God finished speaking to Moses? Exodus 31:18

4. In your own words, describe this sequence of events.

Exodus 32:1–6	
Exodus 32:7–10	
Exodus 32:11–14	
Exodus 32:15–20	
Exodus 32:21–24	
Exodus 32:25–29	

5. Why did the people fall into idolatry? Psalm 106:19–22

— List as many contemporary examples of idolatry as you can find.

Money	*Sex*	*Sports*	*Cars*
Appearance	*Hobbies*	*Fitness*	*Food*
Clothes	*Education*	*Work*	*Fame*
Entertainment			

*Circle the above sources of idolatry that could be a temptation for you!

6. What atonement was made to the Lord? Exodus 32:30–35

7. How was the Lord's anger assuaged? Psalm 106:23

8. Explain the situation in Exodus 33:1–6.

9. What does the column of cloud (Exodus 33:9–10) represent? CCC 697

10. How did God speak to Moses? Exodus 33:11

11. Moses' prayer is characteristic of what type of prayer? CCC 2576

12. Where did Moses find his strength for intercession? CCC 2577

13. What did Moses request of God?

Exodus 33:13	
Exodus 33:15–16	
Exodus 33:18	

14. Describe Moses' relationship with God. Compare your translation with other translations (RSVCE, NAB, JB) from the Bibles of members of your small group.

Exodus 33:12, 17 NAB	
Exodus 33:12, 17 RSVCE	
Exodus 33:12, 17 JB	
Exodus 33:12, 17 other	

15. List two character traits of Moses. Sirach 45:4

16. What can you tell about God's mercy?

Exodus 33:19	
Romans 9:14–15	

17. Can a person see God and live?

Exodus 33:20	
John 1:18	
1 Timothy 6:16	

18. What did the Lord do in Exodus 34:1–9?

19. What happened to Moses' face? Exodus 34:27–35

20. What does Moses' radiant face prefigure? 2 Corinthians 3:12–18

* If you needed prayer, whom would you call upon as an intercessor with you?

CHAPTER 10

The Tent and The Ark
Exodus 35–40

**Then the cloud covered the tent of meeting,
and the glory of the LORD filled the tabernacle.**
Exodus 40:34

The Book of Exodus initially centered on the person of Moses. As the book draws to a close, the genre of writing changes. Increasingly the emphasis now falls on the Torah, the set of instructions given by God through Moses to the people. So the subtitle of the book could be "From Moses to Torah."

"You shall kindle no fire in all your habitations on the sabbath day" (Exodus 35:3). The Third Commandment gives rise to concerns among the people. They ask whether, after they enter into the Promised Land, they will have to rest on the sabbath day even during the busy planting and harvesting seasons (Exodus 34:21). Of more immediate concern is whether they can kindle a fire in their tents on the cold desert nights during their time in the desert, which shall amount to forty years. In reply, Moses clarifies that they may not light a fire on the seventh night, even if that means they will have to wrap themselves in blankets and huddle in their tents.

"And he made for the tent a covering of tanned rams' skins and goatskins" (Exodus 36:19). Chapter 33 mentioned that Moses pitched a special tent well outside the camp (Exodus 33:7). Now chapter 36 describes how the master artisan Bezalel constructed the tent, along with all the other furniture and trappings needed for the Jewish liturgy. The tent comprised three layers of skins: goatskin, ram skin, and "tachash" skin, each layer of eleven pieces stretched in the form of a tent.

The word for tent in Hebrew is *ohel*, which seems to refer to a "peg." The corners of a tent have to be pegged securely into the ground, to prevent desert winds from blowing it away or desert sands from drifting inside. The same word exists in Arabic with the meaning "family"—everyone who lives together in the same tent constitutes a family unit, even if they may be cousins, uncles, aunts, or distant relatives taken in because of need. The fact that Moses shares a tent with God means that God has adopted Moses, and through him the whole people, into a familial relationship.

The Hebrew Bible has four different ways of designating God's tent:

  ❋ Sometimes, just *ha-ohel,* "the tent" (Exodus 33:7)
  ❋ more often, *ohel-mo'ed,* "tent of meeting" (Exodus 33:7b)
  ❋ elsewhere, *ohel-ha'edut,* "tent of testimony" (Numbers 9:15)
  ❋ and in a few places, *ohel-Yahweh,* "tent of the Lord" (1 Kings 2:28-30).

The presence of the tent on the outskirts of the camp is a continuing testimony to the divine presence of Yahweh with His people.

The text never mentions whether Moses pitched the tent of meeting north, south, east, or west of the camp, but without a doubt the direction was to the east. The Israelites have just come out of Egypt, where east is the direction of life. All Egyptian tombs are on the west bank of the Nile, the realm of death. The Israelites find themselves now on a great spiritual journey from the land of slavery in the west. The pillar of cloud by day and the pillar of fire by night, go before them on their eastward journey to the Promised Land. When Moses is in the tent of meeting, the pillar of cloud stands sentinel at the entrance of the tent (Exodus 33:9). Therefore the tent has to be east of the camp.

The entire camp of the Israelites is oriented towards the tent of meeting. The head of each family stands at the entrance of his tent to watch Moses as he goes into the tent (Exodus 33:8), and above his head shines the rising sun. Each individual tent points eastwards, just as the traditional orientation of the Christian liturgy will be toward the east. Tombstones in many traditional Catholic cemeteries also point east, toward the morning sun, as a statement of faith in the general resurrection.

The tent fills the place of a temple in the religion of the nomadic Hebrews. Everything they own has to be portable. For this reason the word temple is never mentioned in the five books of Moses. Psalm 27 reflects this situation: "I will offer in his tent sacrifices with shouts of joy; I will sing and make melody to the Lord." When David fixes his capital at Mount Zion, he erects a tent for the ark there (2 Samuel 6:17). When Solomon dedicates the first temple, he brings the tent into it (1 Kings 8:4). During the centuries when the temple existed, people increasingly regarded it as a central fixture of Judaism. The temple of the Lord obtains significance as the historical resting place for the Mosaic sacred objects, particularly the tent and the ark. During the many centuries when there has been no temple, however, Rabbinic Judaism has defined itself.

"Bezalel made the ark of acacia wood" (Exodus 37:1). In a word association test, mention "ark" and the next word that will come to mind is "Noah." Only later will people think of the ark of the covenant. In Hebrew, however, the two are not even the same word:
* *tebah* = ark of Noah
* *aron* = ark of the covenant

The Septuagint Greek translators rendered both words as *kibotos*. Jerome and the other Latin translators turned both words into *arca* (feminine), which is etymologically related, but not the same as, *arcus* (archer's bow or rainbow). The ark of the covenant was rectangular, but Noah's boat was not.

Noah made his ark of gopherwood, while Bezalel used *shittim* wood, or as we call it, acacia. Common in arid regions, many species of acacia spread through Australia, Asia, Africa, and America. Acacia is the source of gum arabic, harvested for food, medicine, incense, and other practical applications. Middle Eastern craftsmen use acacia in making furniture. The narrow trunks do not yield large boards, and so one piece of furniture may require planks from several trees. The Hebrew text actually says that Bezalel "made the ark of acacia woods" (plural), more than one.

The ark of the covenant may stand less vividly in the collective consciousness, but actually its importance in the Hebrew religion could hardly be overstated. Above that ark was the invisible presence of God from the time of Moses until the disappearance of the ark from history four centuries or so later. Steven Spielberg is praiseworthy for his classic film *Raiders of the Lost Ark*. While wrong in nearly every detail, the film, nonetheless, gives a good general impression.

The actual ark was probably smaller than the one in the film. Exodus gives the dimensions 2.5 x 1.5 x 1.5 cubits, or 45 x 27 x 27 inches, just large enough to hold "a golden urn holding the manna, and Aaron's rod that budded, and the tables of the covenant" (Hebrews 9:4). The Hebrew Bible uses four different phrases to refer to this sacred object:

* sometimes just, *ha-aron,* "the ark" (Exodus 25:10)
* more properly, *aron ha-eadh,* "ark of the testimony" (Exodus 25:22)
* more often, *aron ha-berit,* "ark of the covenant" starting with Numbers 10:33
* elsewhere called, *aron 'uzzeka,* "ark of your might" or strength (Psalm 132:8; 2 Chronicles 6:41).

The ark of the covenant finds mention only twice in the New Testament (Hebrews 9:4 and Revelation 11:19). Of great interest for Mariology (the theology of the Blessed Virgin Mary) is the latter reference: "Then God's temple in heaven was opened, and the ark of his covenant was seen within his temple; and there were flashes of lightning, loud noises, peals of thunder, an earthquake, and heavy hail. And a great portent appeared in heaven, a woman clothed with the sun, with the moon under her feet, and on her head a crown of twelve stars; she was with child" (Revelation 11:19–12:2).

Recall that the dying Jesus entrusted his mother to the care of the beloved disciple, no doubt one of the youngest of His close circle of followers. Every time the apostles saw the elder Mary, they thought of the Person whom she had borne for nine months in her womb. Hence, the ark of the covenant is seen in the Book of Revelation as a type of the Virgin Mother. For this reason, readings about the ark appear on the feasts of Mary, especially on the feast of the Assumption of Mary into heaven on August 15th.

"And he made a mercy seat of pure gold" (Exodus 37:6). The mercy seat, called in Greek the *hilasteron* (Romans 3:25; Hebrews 9:5), and in some modern translations the "propitiatory," is God's own earthly throne. No one sat in the mercy seat except the invisible God alone. The empty chair is an important theme in the Jewish religion. At every Passover meal, one seat is left empty for the Prophet Elijah, who will return one day, just before the Messiah.

The mercy seat finds mention in only three books of the Hebrew Bible (Exodus [16 times], Leviticus [5 times], and Numbers [only once at Numbers 7:89]). Saint Paul identifies Jesus Christ with the mercy seat, which God appointed "as an expiation by his blood, to be received by faith" (Romans 3:25). The appearance of the technical term *hilasterion,* seems not to be noticed by translators.

Since the First Commandment forbade the formation of images to represent the Divine, the closest thing possible in Judaism is an empty space, the space above the mercy seat. Some religions (Islam, and certain branches of Christianity) forbid any and all representational art, but they do not seem to notice the angels that appear on either side of the empty space above the mercy seat.

"And he made two cherubim of hammered gold" (Exodus 37:7). The general word for angel in Hebrew is *mal'ach,* as in the verse, "And I will send an angel before you" (Exodus 33:2). Angels appear practically everywhere in the Bible, from the first book (Genesis 3:24) to the last (Revelation 22:16).

Special kinds of angels are the cherubim and the seraphim. The *–im* ending indicates the plural in Hebrew. More than one cherub is a group of *cherubim*; more than one seraph are *seraphim.*

The Prophet Isaiah has the only sighting of seraphim in the Bible, when he sees God in heaven: "Above him stood the seraphim; each had six wings: with two he covered his face, and with two he covered his feet, and with two he flew. And one called to another and said: Holy, holy, holy is the Lord of hosts; the whole earth is full of his glory" (Isaiah 6:2–3). This passage becomes the Sanctus of the Mass.

The Prophet Ezekiel, on the other hand, has a vision of the cherubim of God (Ezekiel 10:5–20 and 41:18–25), and describes them in this way: "Each had four faces, and each four wings, and underneath their wings the semblance of human hands" (Ezekiel 10:21). In Ezekiel's vision each cherub has four wings, while in Isaiah's vision each seraph has six wings.

Cherubim appear more frequently than seraphim in the Bible, starting with the Book of Exodus, when Bezalel fashions two of them of pure gold attached to either side of the mercy seat atop the ark. The cherubim help to frame the empty space above the seat that is inhabited by God and God alone. The cherubim are like horns to the saddle of God when He sits on top of the ark. One of the important Davidic psalms says that God "rode upon a cherub, and flew; he was seen upon the wings of the wind" (Psalm 18:10, 2 Samuel 22:11).

Since two golden angels appear on either side of the invisible God atop the ark, the Mosaic liturgy cannot be described as iconoclastic, or against all kinds of religious art. Indeed, later Solomon adorns the temple in Jerusalem with two gigantic "cherubim carved from olivewood and covered with gold, each ten cubits high" (1 Kings 6:23), which would be fifteen feet tall. Smaller cherubim appear engraved on the surrounding walls (1 Kings 6:29). Solomon's bronze stands have carved panels, "and on the panels that were set in the frames were lions, oxen, and cherubim" (1 Kings 7:29).

God did not forbid religious art. Neither Moses nor Solomon forbade any and all representational art. The First Commandment bans objects to be worshipped as false gods, but not objects that assist in the worship of the One, True God. As the angels and saints worship God continually in heaven, we can use their images to help focus our minds during our earthly prayers of adoration.

HOLY GOD, WE PRAISE THY NAME

Holy God, we praise thy name; Lord of all we bow before thee!
All on earth thy scepter claim, all in heaven above adore thee;
Infinite, thy vast domain, everlasting is thy reign.
Infinite, thy vast domain, everlasting is thy reign.

Hark! The loud celestial hymn angel choirs above are raising;
Cherubim and Seraphim, in unceasing chorus praising;
Fill the heavens with sweet accord: "Holy, holy, holy Lord!"
Fill the heavens with sweet accord: "Holy, holy, holy Lord!"

Holy Father, Holy Son, Holy Spirit, Three we name thee;
While in essence only One, undivided God we claim thee;
And adoring, bend the knee, while we own the mystery.
And adoring, bend the knee, while we own the mystery.

Paraphrase of Te Deum Laudamus,
ascribed to Saint Nicetas of Remesiana (AD 335–414).

1. Explain the Sabbath regulations given in Exodus 35:1–3.

2. Assign a title to each of the following sections of Scripture.

Exodus 35:4–9	
Exodus 35:10–19	
Exodus 35:20–29	
Exodus 35:30–35	

3. What were some of the characteristics of Bezalel and Oholiab? Exodus 36:1–3

4. How generous were the Israelites? Exodus 36:3–7

5. In what specific ways could you be more generous to the Lord with your time, talent, and treasure?

6. Draw or briefly describe the tabernacle. Exodus 36:8–38

7. What was present in the Old Testament ark? CCC 2058

8. What is the purpose and ideal placement of the tabernacle today?

CCC 1183	
CCC 1379	

9. What is described in the following passages?

Exodus 37:6	
Romans 3:21–25	
Hebrews 9:1–5	

10. Describe a time in your life when you have experienced God's mercy.

11. Write a short phrase to name what is described in these passages.

Exodus 37:1–9	
Exodus 37:10–16	
Exodus 37:17–24	
Exodus 37:25–29	

12. What and who do you see in the following passages?

Revelation 11:19	
Revelation 12:1–6	

13. From the Litany of the Blessed Virgin Mary (Litany of Loreto) pp. 105–106, list titles of the Blessed Mother that come from terms found in Exodus 36–40.

14. What structures are described in these passages?

Exodus 38:1–8	
Exodus 38:9–20	

15. List some of the precious metals the Israelites used. Exodus 38:24–31

16. What was made for the priests in Exodus 39:1–31?

17. What do Catholic priests wear for liturgy today?

18. What happened when the work was completed? Exodus 39:42–43

19. What happened when the tent and the ark were completed? Exodus 40

20. Spend some time before the tabernacle this week, and meditate on God's presence and mercy. What helps you to focus on the magnificence of God?

Litany of the Blessed Virgin Mary
(Litany of Loreto)

Lord, have mercy.	*Lord, have mercy.*
Christ, have mercy.	*Christ, have mercy.*
Christ, hear us.	*Christ, graciously hear us.*
God, the Father of heaven,	*have mercy on us.*
God, the Son, redeemer of the world,	*have mercy on us.*
God, the Holy Spirit,	*have mercy on us.*
Holy Mary,	*pray for us.*
Holy Mother of God,	*pray for us.*
Holy Virgin of Virgins,	*pray for us.*
Mother of Christ,	*pray for us.*
Mother of divine grace,	*pray for us.*
Mother most pure,	*pray for us.*
Mother most chaste,	*pray for us.*
Mother inviolate,	*pray for us.*
Mother undefiled,	*pray for us.*
Mother most lovable,	*pray for us.*
Mother most admirable,	*pray for us.*
Mother of good counsel,	*pray for us.*
Mother of our creator,	*pray for us.*
Mother of our Savior,	*pray for us.*
Virgin most prudent,	*pray for us.*
Virgin most venerable,	*pray for us.*
Virgin most renowned,	*pray for us.*
Virgin most powerful,	*pray for us.*
Virgin most merciful,	*pray for us.*
Virgin most faithful,	*pray for us.*
Mirror of justice,	*pray for us.*
Seat of wisdom,	*pray for us.*
Cause of our joy,	*pray for us.*
Spiritual vessel,	*pray for us.*
Vessel of honor,	*pray for us.*
Singular vessel of devotion,	*pray for us.*
Mystical rose,	*pray for us.*
Tower of David,	*pray for us.*
Tower of ivory,	*pray for us.*
House of gold,	*pray for us.*

Ark of the covenant,	*pray for us.*
Gate of heaven,	*pray for us.*
Morning star,	*pray for us.*
Health of the sick,	*pray for us.*
Refuge of sinners,	*pray for us.*
Comfort of the afflicted,	*pray for us.*
Help of Christians,	*pray for us.*
Queen of angels,	*pray for us.*
Queen of patriarchs,	*pray for us.*
Queen of prophets,	*pray for us.*
Queen of apostles,	*pray for us.*
Queen of martyrs,	*pray for us.*
Queen of confessors,	*pray for us.*
Queen of virgins,	*pray for us.*
Queen of all saints,	*pray for us.*
Queen conceived without original sin,	*pray for us.*
Queen assumed into heaven,	*pray for us.*
Queen of the most holy rosary,	*pray for us.*
Queen of peace,	*pray for us.*

Lamb of God,
    you take away the sins of the world,   *spare us, O Lord.*

Lamb of God,
    you take away the sins of the world,   *graciously, hear us,*
    O Lord.

Lamb of God,
    you take away the sins of the world,   *have mercy on us.*

Pray for us, O holy Mother of God.

    That we may be made worthy
    of the promises of Christ.

Let us pray: Grant that we your servants, Lord, may enjoy unfailing health of mind and body, and through the prayers of the ever Blessed Virgin Mary in her glory, free us from our sorrows in this world and give us eternal happiness in the next. Through Christ our Lord. *Amen.*

CHAPTER 11

The Levitical Priesthood
Leviticus 1–16

**Then Moses said to Aaron, "This is what the LORD has said,
'I will show myself holy among those who are near me,
and before all the people I will be glorified.'"
And Aaron held his peace.**
Leviticus 10:3

The Holiness of God — Probably you will not find many people who claim Leviticus as their favorite book of the Bible. With its detailed directives for the liturgical rituals of the Levitical priesthood for animal sacrifice and other Jewish religious practices that have been abandoned since the destruction of the Temple in Jerusalem in AD 70, it can pose very difficult reading for a contemporary Christian. Nonetheless, if you peer beneath the exterior, you will find an attempt to focus on the absolute perfect, mysterious, unfathomable, holiness of God.

Of the 613 commandments found in Scripture, 247 of those laws, more than one third, are found in the book of Leviticus. The theological underpinnings of the book of Leviticus provide a rich source of inspiration for New Testament writers, particularly the writer of the Letter to the Hebrews. The Levitical priesthood pre-figures the perfect high priesthood of Jesus, which is far superior to that of Aaron.

Indeed, under the law almost everything is purified with blood, and without the shedding of blood there is no forgiveness of sins. Thus it was necessary for the copies of the heavenly things to be purified with these rites, but the heavenly things themselves with better sacrifices than these. For Christ has entered, not into a sanctuary made with hands, a copy of the true one, but into heaven itself, now to appear in the presence of God on our behalf. Nor was it to offer himself repeatedly, as the high priest enters the Holy Place yearly with blood not his own; for then he would have had to suffer repeatedly since the foundation of the world. But as it is, he has appeared once for all at the end of the age to put away sin by the sacrifice of himself. And just as it is appointed for men to die once, and after that comes judgment, so Christ, having been offered once to bear the sins of many, will appear a second time, not to deal with sin but to save those who eagerly wait for him.

Hebrews 9:22–28

Underlying the book of Leviticus is the truth that God really dwells with His people. The all-holy God dwells in the midst of the people. God is holy, pure, clean, mysterious, and powerful. The concept of the sacred is an idea that contemporary society would do well to re-visit. The idea of a group of people entrusted with preserving a sacred space for the Lord has applications for all God-fearing people of all times. God is a God of order and preference. God prefers that people relate to Him in specific ways, not any old way. Rather than seeing man created in the image and likeness of God, society has created a false god created in man's image. So, people say things like "God doesn't care what I wear, as long as I am here," or "God doesn't really care about this." In this way, contemporary man seeks to fashion an imaginary god according to his own preferences.

Leviticus teaches something quite different. God is a God of order. God mandates an exact order of how worship and liturgy should be conducted. The sanctuary, God's dwelling place, and the source of holiness and blessing is the central focal point. The Holy of Holies, where God's divine presence appears above the ark, is in the center and is the Most Holy Place. The court is less holy, and then the camp follows. The High Priest is expected to be the most holy person, with the Levitical priests following in holiness after him, and then the people following the priests.

"And this is the law of the sacrifice of peace offerings which one may offer to the Lord" (Leviticus 7:11). There are many offerings prescribed for various situations in the everyday life of the Chosen People. Holocausts are animal sacrifices of pure, unblemished animals that are slaughtered before the Lord. There are cereal offerings, sin offerings, peace offerings, thank offerings, offerings for personal, collective, and inadvertent sins. The priests offered guilt offerings on behalf of the people. Sometimes the people were aware of the sins they had committed against Almighty God. At other times, they offered sacrifice because they may have offended God unintentionally. The people understood that they were to accept their guilt and make atonement for their sins, even when they were not entirely culpable. This is in stark contrast with present day society, in which someone or something else is frequently blamed for anyone's weakness or transgression.

Despite the heavy emphasis on sacrifice in Leviticus, the Old Testament clearly teaches that perfect obedience to God's commands pleases Him far more than sacrifices to atone for disobedience. The prophet Samuel tried to teach this lesson to King Saul, after Saul failed to obey God's commands implicitly.

> Has the LORD as great delight in burnt offerings and sacrifices,
>> as in obeying the voice of the LORD?
> Behold, to obey is better than sacrifice,
>> and to hearken than the fat of rams.
> For rebellion is as the sin of divination,
>> and stubbornness is as iniquity and idolatry.
>> 1 Samuel 15:22–23

Moreover, the prayers in the Book of Psalms clearly show that the condition of a person's heart is of utmost importance to the all-holy God. God explains to the people that although sacrifices are required, they actually do nothing for God. Animal sacrifices in and of themselves cannot atone for sin or make a sufficient restitution to Almighty God. Despite the fact that sacrifices are prescribed, they are not adequate. Man cannot give to God anything that God doesn't already own.

> I will accept no bull from your house,
> > nor he-goat from your folds.
> For every beast of the forest is mine,
> > the cattle on a thousand hills.
> I know all the birds of the air,
> > and all that moves in the field is mine.
> If I were hungry, I would not tell you;
> > for the world and all that is in it is mine.
> Do I eat the flesh of bulls,
> > or drink the blood of goats?
> Offer to God a sacrifice of thanksgiving,
> > and pay your vows to the Most High;
> and call upon me in the day of trouble;
> > I will deliver you, and you shall glorify me.
>
> Psalm 50:9–15

Clearly God does not need the sacrifices man needs to offer. But, God prescribes a set of rituals to teach man the difference between the acceptable and unacceptable, the difference between the sacred and the profane.

In Psalm 51, the psalmist acknowledges what is truly pleasing to Almighty God. "For thou hast no delight in sacrifice; were I to give a burnt offering, thou would not be pleased. The sacrifice acceptable to God is a contrite spirit; a broken and contrite heart, O God, thou wilt not despise" (Psalm 51:16–17). Like the Old Testament people, you might offer to God a sacrifice of prayer, alms, fasting, or self-denial. Yet, without a pure heart and a repentant spirit, these outward sacrifices may be of little avail. Even in the Old Testament, God teaches that the condition of the heart must be considered before the sacrifice being offered.

"And you shall not go out from the door of the tent of meeting for seven days, until the days of your ordination are completed, for it will take seven days to ordain you" (Leviticus 8:33). God mandated the ordination ceremony for Aaron and the Levitical priests in a very detailed fashion. The seven days of the ordination ceremony correspond with the six days of creation (Genesis 1:1–2:3), followed by a day of divine rest. Therefore, worship according to the priestly view of creation could then begin on the eighth day.

It should be pointed out that the Levitical priesthood is something entirely different than the Sacrament of Holy Orders conferred on Catholic priests today. The Levitical priesthood was passed on along family lines. If you were a son of Aaron, you were automatically in the priestly tribe of Levi. This brought some problems along with it. A holy father did not always raise reverent sons. This becomes apparent in the horrible episode of the sons of Aaron offering unholy or profane fire, resulting in their deaths. We cannot determine the exact nature of their disobedience. What we can determine clearly is that God gave specific directives to them, and Nadab and Abihu did something else. Perhaps they thought it was "no big deal." Obviously, God saw the situation differently.

Later, when King David was bringing the ark of God back to Jerusalem, Uzzah reached out to steady the ark, which the oxen were tipping. When Uzzah touched the holy ark, God became angry with him. Uzzah died on the spot (2 Samuel 6:1ff). Apparently, God was repeatedly trying to teach the people the seriousness of the holy, and the importance of the sacred. What is set apart for God, must not be treated too casually.

Today, the priests are the custodians of the sacred space that we set aside for God in our churches. The priest is the guardian of the Blessed Sacrament. He is responsible for the tabernacle and the most holy place. Lay people should remember and teach the children that God's house is a holy place. People enter reverently. Food and drink is left outside. Worshipers dress carefully. The architecture of many church buildings can pose challenges today. Sometimes the parish hall, or social rooms are adjacent to the church. People may be talking and socializing, while others are trying to pray and to worship. The tragic examples of Nadab and Abihu, and Uzzah may provide an application for Christians today.

The Catholic priesthood is not a Levitical priesthood. Rather, the Catholic priest functions in the person of Christ, *in persona Christi*. Jesus was not a Levite. Jesus came from the tribe of Judah, and therefore was ineligible for the Levitical priesthood. "So also Christ did not exalt himself to be made a high priest, but was appointed by him who said to him, 'Thou art my Son, today I have begotten thee'; as he says also in another place 'Thou art a priest for ever, after the order of Melchizedek'" (Hebrews 5:5–6, quoting Psalm 110:4). The Levitical priesthood was biologically ordained according to tribal ancestry. The priesthood of Jesus Christ is a charismatic priesthood, a divine selection and anointing by God.

Despite the differences in the priestly offices, Saint Thomas Aquinas in his *Summa Theologiae* found an interpretation in the high priest's vestments that could be applicable to priests today. First the gold plate on the forehead of the high priest should help the priest to remember God in contemplation. Next, the ephod worn on the shoulders of the high priest reminds the priest that he bears the weakness of the people. Thirdly, the breastplate should remind the priest to keep the people in his heart with charitable concern. Fourthly, the violet robe signifies that the priest's manner of life should be heavenly in the perfection of his daily activities.

Perhaps in reading about Moses anointing Aaron with the holy oil of priesthood, it would be good to meditate on Psalm 133:1–2.

> Behold, how good and pleasant it is when brothers dwell in unity!
> It is like the precious oil upon the head, running down upon the beard,
> Upon the beard of Aaron, running down on the collar of his robes!
>
> Psalm 133:1–2

1–5. Identify the types of offerings described in each section below.

Leviticus 1	
Leviticus 2	
Leviticus 3	
Leviticus 4:1–12	
Leviticus 4:13–21	
Leviticus 4:22–26	
Leviticus 5:14ff	
Leviticus 6:1–6	
Leviticus 6:7–16	
Leviticus 6:17–23	
Leviticus 7:1–10	
Leviticus 7:11–21	

* Have you ever made a special offering to the Lord for a specific situation?

6. Find a common thread in the following verses.

Leviticus 5:4	
1 Samuel 14:24	
Mark 6:22–26	
Acts 23:12	

7. What significance can you find in the passages below?

Leviticus 5:7	
Luke 2:22–24	

8. Describe the ordination ceremony for Aaron and his sons. Leviticus 8

9. What can you learn from these verses?

Leviticus 6:23 NAB Leviticus 6:30 RSVCE	
Hebrews 9:22	
Hebrews 13:11–12	
CCC 433	

10. Compare the following passages.

Leviticus 8:12	
Psalm 133	
Sirach 45:15–16	

11. What happened after the ordination ceremony? Leviticus 9:22–24

12. Describe the drama in the following passages.

Leviticus 10:1–5	
Leviticus 10:6–11	
Leviticus 10:12–20	

13. List some clean and unclean foods. Leviticus 11:1–47

Clean	Unclean

14. Compare the following verses.

Leviticus 11:44	
Matthew 5:48	
1 Peter 1:16	

15. What was prescribed for a woman after childbirth? Leviticus 12

16. Leviticus chapters 13–14 concerns what?

17. Describe some contemporary conditions, which sound similar to the examples of uncleanness from Leviticus 15.

18. Compare the following passages.

Leviticus 16:1–19	
Hebrews 9:3–12	

19. What can you learn from the following passages?

Leviticus 16:21–22	
Isaiah 53:4–6, 10–12	
John 1:29	
1 Peter 2:24	

20. List one unclean practice that you could eliminate from your life to purify yourself and become more holy before the Lord.

**List one positive habit you could practice to become more holy for the Lord?

CHAPTER 12

Holiness
Leviticus 17–22

You shall be holy; for I the LORD your God am holy.
Leviticus 19:2

God expects that His people should be holy, because He is perfect holiness. Leviticus offers practical instructions for living in ways that are pleasing to God, and for avoiding behaviors that offend the all-holy God. This section of Sacred Scripture could be seen as a holiness code, or a type of handbook for holiness. These instructive passages deal with many aspects of human relationships, worship that is acceptable to God, and social justice.

God's holiness transcends human understanding, inspiring God-fearing people to emulate His holiness with respect and awe. God does not merely call for piety in one's private life, or reverent worship on the sabbath. Rather, God demands holiness as a way of life, penetrating every aspect of personal, family, social, and civic relationships. In conforming oneself to God's directives, a person finds meaning in life and contentment. Obedience to God allows one to grow in holiness. Disobedience to God separates one from holiness and leads one to become profane.

> The pious Jew prayed daily the words of the Book of Deuteronomy which expressed the heart of his existence: "Hear, O Israel: the LORD our God is one LORD, and you shall love the LORD your God with all your heart, and with all your soul and with all your might" (Deuteronomy 6:4–5). Jesus united into a single precept this commandment of love for God and the commandment of love for neighbor found in the Book of Leviticus: "You shall love your neighbor as yourself" (Leviticus 19:18; cf. Mark 12:29–31). Since God first loved us (cf. 1 John 4:10), love is no longer a mere "command;" it is the response to the gift of love with which God draws near to us.
> Pope Benedict XVI, *Deus Caritas Est* (December 25, 2005), 1.

"For the life of every creature is its blood" (Leviticus 17:14). Life is the divine prerogative, because God is the author and origin of life. Blood is a symbol of life. When a human being or an animal bleeds, it becomes weaker and weaker, until it becomes lifeless and dies. Animal sacrifice, as an atonement for sin or as an offering to God, was part of the tradition of Israel. Moses says that sacrifice is to be brought to the altar of the Lord in the sanctuary. This prefigures the perfect sacrifice of the blood of Jesus Christ offered for the redemption of sinners (Romans 3:22–26). But, God forbids the offering of sacrifice to satyrs, which were a type of goat in the wilderness, believed to have demonic attributes. All idolatry is sinful, but sacrificing to evil is a form of idolatry, which is especially abhorrent to God (Leviticus 17:7).

People in pagan cultures drank blood. They believed, that the life and attributes of the victim, would be assumed by the one who drank the blood. Such practices may have continued up to the early Church, causing the elders at the Council of Jerusalem to advise Christian converts to abstain from blood (Acts 15:13–20).

The Sacredness of Sex — Since God is the author of life, creating man and woman in His own likeness, human sexuality is His domain and His prerogative. The complementarity of a man and a woman for the purpose of procreation and unification is part of the divine blueprint. A married couple, cooperating with God's grace, and submitting to His command to be fruitful and multiply, enjoys special graces and blessings. Holiness demands conformity to God's divine plan.

> The unity of which Genesis 2:24 speaks—"they become one flesh"—is undoubtedly expressed and realized in the conjugal act. The biblical formulation, extremely concise and simple, indicates sex, femininity and masculinity, as that characteristic of man—male and female—which permits them, when they become "one flesh," to submit their whole humanity to the blessing of fertility. However, the whole context of the lapidary formulation does not permit us to stop at the surface of human sexuality. It does not allow us to deal with the body and sex outside the full dimension of man and of the "communion of persons." Right from the beginning it obliges us to see the fullness and depth which are characteristic of this unity, which man and woman must constitute in the light of the revelation of the body.
> Pope John Paul II, *The Theology of the Body*
> (Boston, MA: Pauline Books, 1997), p. 49.

Leviticus gives specific and comprehensive restrictions for sexual activity. Twelve prohibitions forbid sexual relations between family members. Today, centuries after these prohibitions were given, the majority of child sexual abuse cases still occur in the home. Children still need to be protected from the uncontrolled impulses of siblings and adult relatives. Sexual intercourse must still be reserved for within the marital relationship. The prohibition against adultery strives to preserve the marital union and protect the children of the family.

Child sacrifice is strictly forbidden by God. Archeological digs in Gezer unearthed the remains of children sacrificed to the pagan god, Molech. In Jerusalem, children were burned in the valley of Ben-Hinnom (2 Kings 16:3, 21:6, Jeremiah 7:31). Later, in Jesus' time, a garbage dump at this site continually burned stinking refuse. Jesus used this site at Gehenna to explain the fires of hell (Mark 9:42–48).

God warns the people to remove sexual impropriety from their midst and to expel sexual deviants from the community. God is pure and holy, and He demands that His people be pure and holy as well. Sexuality is such a powerful gift from God that it comes with serious responsibility to preserve its goodness.

"You shall not lie with a male as with a woman; it is an abomination" (Leviticus 19:22). Homosexuality is a sin against nature. A sexual act outside of God's order transgresses the boundaries that God has prescribed. While homosexual acts are sinful and can never be accepted, homosexual desires and inclinations, while disordered, are not sins. The Roman Catholic Church recognizes the inherent human dignity of each and every person created in the image and likeness of God.

The Catholic Church offers support and encouragement for individuals who experience homosexual impulses and yet desire to live a chaste and holy life. **Courage** is an apostolate of the church which ministers to those with same sex attractions of any denomination. **Encourage** specifically ministers to the relatives and friends of persons with same sex attractions. They can be reached at http://couragerc.net or NYCourage@aol.com or at (212) 268-1010.

> Homosexual acts are intrinsically disordered. They are contrary to the natural law. They close the sexual act to the gift of life. They do not proceed from a genuine affective and sexual complementarity. Under no circumstances can they be approved.   CCC 2357
>
> Homosexual persons are called to chastity. By the virtues of self-mastery that teach them inner freedom, at times by the support of disinterested friendship, by prayer and sacramental grace, they can and should gradually and resolutely approach Christian perfection.   CCC 2359
>
> They must be accepted with respect, compassion, and sensitivity.   CCC 2358

Holiness requires that each individual conform to the role assigned by God. There will be temptations to act outside of God's perfect plan and will. Growth in virtue and holiness occur when we cooperate with God's grace and allow God's grace to change us. Some persons long to be married, but cannot find a suitable partner. Some married persons must forego sexual activity because of the illness of a spouse or a separation due to business travel or military service. Some individuals take a vow of celibacy to make themselves totally available to the service of the Lord and His Church. No one can act on every sexual impulse or desire. Everyone must learn self-discipline. Sexual relations must be reserved for within the marriage bed.

"You shall be holy, for I the Lord am holy" (Leviticus 19:2). Holiness is an attribute of God that He wants to pass on to His children. It becomes the fabric and pattern of life. God loves the poor and expects people to take a concern for the poor out of love for Him. All are strangers and sojourners. Everyone is just passing through this land on the way to an eternal homeland. Before a perfect God, every man is a poor, undeserving beggar, pleading for mercy.

Holiness is manifest in practical ways. Civic responsibility demands honesty and respect for property. Social justice requires fair labor practices. One must give an honest day's work for an honest day's wage. The employer must take a concern for the needs and dignity of the worker. The employer must not mistreat the worker, nor withhold his wages. The worker is also held to high standards.

> The human rights that flow from work are part of the broader context of those fundamental rights of the person. ... A policy is correct when the objective rights of the worker are fully respected.
> Pope John Paul II, *Laborem Exercens* (September 14, 1981), 16.1, 17.1.

No partiality is to be shown to the rich or the poor, but justice and righteousness should prevail. Special concern should be given to the deaf, the blind, the elderly, and the stranger. Proper respect should be given to those who are vulnerable, those who are advanced in years, and particularly, those of one's own family.

While avoiding the sinful behaviors that scripture warns one to resist, holiness also requires one to be proactive. It is not enough to simply avoid sinful behaviors, one must use God's grace to do good. Someone may not be doing anything particularly wrong, but he may not be doing anything good either. To become holy, as God is holy, requires obedience to the commands of God. One must avoid the evil he must not do, while at the same time embracing the good that God desires.

Leviticus also warns against witchcraft, mediums, and wizards, which can be reflected in the present age by fascination with horoscopes, Ouija boards, palm readers, fortune-tellers, and practitioners of Wicca. Dabbling in the domain of evil is a dangerous practice that should be seriously avoided. Parents must be rigorous in screening the games and activities that young people may explore, which can lead them into the realm of darkness, which is incompatible with the holiness of God.

The Bible speaks clearly about duties and responsibilities. These commands may seem harsh and foreign to those who live in a culture preoccupied with rights, privileges, and pleasures. An appropriate understanding of the dignity of the human person, created in the image and likeness of a loving God who desires each of His children to live with Him forever in heaven, makes striving for holiness the prime objective in life. It is in obedience to God's commands that one finds true joy.

> **Keep the joy of loving God in your heart**
> **and share this joy with all you meet, especially your family. Be holy.**
>
> **Blessed Mother Teresa of Calcutta**
> **(August 26, 1910—September 5, 1997)**

1. What is the main focus of Leviticus 17:1–9?

2. What common idea runs through these passages?

Leviticus 17:11	
Ephesians 1:7, 2:13	
Hebrews 13:10–12	

3. Identify the family relationships in which sex is forbidden.

Leviticus 18:7	
Leviticus 18:8	*Step-mother*
Leviticus 18:9	
Leviticus 18:10	
Leviticus 18:12	
Leviticus 18:13	*Maternal aunt*
Leviticus 18:15	
Leviticus 18:16	
Leviticus 18:17	
Leviticus 18:18	

4. Name the sin found in Leviticus 18:20 and Exodus 20:14.

5. What does the Bible say about homosexual acts?

Leviticus 18:22	
Leviticus 20:13	
Romans 1:26–28	
1 Corinthians 6:9–11	

6. Explain Catholic Church teaching on homosexual relations?   CCC 2357

7. Persons with same sex attraction should do what? CCC 2358

8. With prayer and grace, what can a homosexual person achieve? CCC 2359

9. What can result from defilement? Leviticus 18:22–30

10. What does God expect of you?

Leviticus 19:2	
Leviticus 20:7, 26	
Matthew 5:48	
1 Peter 1:14–16	

11. Who is called to holiness? CCC 2013

12. How can holiness be achieved? CCC 2014, 2015

13. What should be done for the poor? Leviticus 19:9–10

* Can you do something for the poor this week? Could you serve in a soup kitchen, donate food to a food pantry, or give some money to a relief organization?

14. Identify the prohibitions in the following verses.

Leviticus 19:11	
Leviticus 19:12	
Leviticus 19:13	
Leviticus 19:14	
Leviticus 19:15	
Leviticus 19:16	

15. Compare the following passages.

Leviticus 19:18	
Matthew 5:43–44	
Luke 10:27	

16. What common practice is discussed in Leviticus 19:28?

17. Find a common theme in the following verses.

Leviticus 19:26, 31	
Leviticus 20:6, 27	

18. Read Leviticus 21 and give a title to the chapter.

19. Read Leviticus 22 and assign a title to the chapter.

20. What practical things could you do this week to heed God's commands and bring more holiness into your daily life?

__ *Prayer*   __ *Kind deeds (describe)*

__ *Adoration of the Blessed Sacrament*   __ *Forgive someone*

__ *Restore a broken relationship*   __ *Give something to the poor*

__ *Confession*   ___ *Other, please explain*

Monthly Social Activity

This month, your small group will meet for coffee, tea, or a simple breakfast, lunch, or dessert in someone's home. Pray for this social event and for the host or hostess. Try, if at all possible, to attend.

After a short prayer and some time for small talk, write one sentence about a person you know personally who is an example of holiness to you. You can mention a famous person but also talk about someone in your family, your neighborhood, or your parish, who is striving to live a holy life and giving a good example of holiness.

Examples:

◆ *My grandmother loved God and prayed for me. She encouraged me to seek out God's perfect will for my life.*

◆ *My Dad was always helping people who were in need. He gave work to people in need, taught them how to do things, and paid them.*

◆ *Arthur in the parish brought Holy Communion to me when I was recovering from surgery.*

CHAPTER 13

Feasts and Offerings
Leviticus 23–27

**And I will walk among you, and will be your God,
And you shall be my people.**
Leviticus 26:12

Just as God created time and seasons for the world, He ordained sacred times of rest and celebration, to set apart the people of God from the secular world around them. At the beginning of Genesis, God revealed the order of creation unfolding in a six day, period of time, with the seventh day being a day of rest. In Genesis, God had already prescribed the sabbath as a day of rest, but now, here in Leviticus 23:1–3, God further instructs that the seventh day is also a time for holy convocation, or worship, as well as a sabbath of solemn rest. Not only are God's people expected to refrain from work on the sabbath, but they should also come together to worship the Lord.

Creation is oriented to the sabbath, which is the sign of the covenant between God and humankind. Creation is designed in such a way that it is oriented to worship. It fulfills its purpose and assumes its significance when it is lived, ever new, with a view to worship. Creation exists for the sake of worship. The true center, the power that moves and shapes from within in the rhythm of the stars and of our lives, is worship. Our life's rhythm moves in proper measure when it is caught up in this. …

The Bible declares that creation has its structure in the sabbath ordinance. But the sabbath is in its turn the summing up of Torah, the law of Israel. This means that worship has a moral aspect to it. God's whole moral order has been taken up into it; only thus is it truly worship. To this must be added the fact that Torah, the law, is an expression of Israel's history with God. It is an expression of the covenant, and the covenant is an expression of God's love, of His "yes" to the human being that He created, so that He could both love and receive love. …

In the creation account the sabbath is depicted as the day when the human being, in the freedom of worship, participates in God's freedom, in God's rest, and thus in God's peace. To celebrate the sabbath means to celebrate the covenant. It means to return to the source and to sweep away all the defilement that our work has brought with it.

Pope Benedict XVI, *In the Beginning*
(Grand Rapids, MI: Eerdmans, 1995), pp. 27–31.

The orientation of the human spirit is directed toward worship. When one encounters beauty in the world—a beautiful sunrise, a rainbow, the pattern of clouds, a spectacular sunset, the birth of a child, the sound of music or laughter, one wants to express praise and gratitude. Pity the soul that experiences beauty, but has no one to praise and thank for it. God reveals to His people the appointed times and specific structure for feasts and festivals. In addition to the Sabbath, which occurs every seventh day, the Jewish calendar also includes moveable feasts that can occur on any day of the week including three great pilgrimage feasts.

The Feasts of Passover, *Pesach,* **and Unleavened Bread,** (Leviticus 23:5–8) combined to form the first great pilgrimage feast, celebrated in the springtime, beginning in the evening of the fourteenth day of the first month, Nisan (March–April). Passover commemorated God's deliverance of the Chosen People from their time of slavery in Egypt (Exodus 12–13). The re-telling of the events of the Exodus became part of the Passover ritual, along with the sacrifice of a perfect, unblemished lamb. Unleavened bread was an agricultural feast in the springtime reaping of the barley harvest, to honor the Lord of the harvest, which continued for seven days.

The Synoptics identify the Last Super that Jesus shared with His apostles as a Passover meal. According to John's Gospel, Jesus was crucified at the time when the Passover lambs were being slaughtered in the Temple. Just as the Passover lamb was to be eaten whole without breaking its legs, the soldiers did not break Jesus' legs (John 19:33). John the Baptist identifies Jesus as the Lamb of God when he says: "Behold, the Lamb of God who takes away the sin of the world" (John 1:29).

Saint Paul recalls the feast of Unleavened Bread when he calls Christians to a life of holiness. "Cleanse out the old leaven that you may be new dough, as you really are un-leavened. For Christ, our Paschal Lamb, has been sacrificed. Let us, therefore, celebrate the festival, not with the old leaven, the leaven of malice and evil, but the with the un-leavened bread of sincerity and truth" (1 Corinthians 5:7–8).

The Feast of Weeks, *Shabbathoth,* (Leviticus 23:15–22), the second Harvest Festival and second great pilgrimage feast, celebrated the first fruits of the harvest, seven weeks after the feast of Unleavened Bread in the late spring. Counting the first and last days of the feast, there are fifty days. The Greek word, *Pentekoste,* means fiftieth, referring to the fiftieth day, and from this comes the word Pentecost. During this feast, sacrifices of sin offerings and peace offerings were prescribed in atonement for sin, and in thanksgiving to God for blessing the people. Later, this feast of Pentecost also commemorated Moses receiving the law on Mount Sinai fifty days after the exodus (Exodus 19:1).

Jesus, as a faithful and observant Jew, celebrated all the prescribed feasts and festivals of the Jewish people. During His lifetime, Jesus promised that He would send a Counselor, the Spirit of Truth, the Holy Spirit (John 14:15–30). After Jesus' Ascension into heaven, the Holy Spirit descended upon the apostles on the day of Pentecost, as Jesus promised. Tongues of fire rested on each, and they were filled with Holy Spirit, and began to speak in other tongues (Acts 2:1–4). The Jewish feast of Pentecost anticipated the Christian feast of Pentecost, during which the gifts and the fruit of the Holy Spirit would be poured out on the Church.

The Feast of Trumpets, or Day of Acclamation (Leviticus 23:23–25), was a holy day celebrated on the first day of the seventh month, Tishri (September–October) in autumn. All work stopped at this time, and silver trumpets were blown for the Lord. At one time, this feast may have honored God as the creator and king. This feast is now known as *Rosh Hashanna* or Jewish New Year.

The Day of Atonement, in Hebrew *Yom Kippur,* (Leviticus 23:26–32) was celebrated nine days later on the tenth day of the seventh month, Tishri. Along with the command to refrain from work, this feast was a day of national fasting and penance for sin, afflicting oneself and offering atonement to God, from evening of one day to the evening of the next.

The Feast of Booths, in Hebrew *Sukkoth,* also called Tabernacles, or Ingathering was the third annual pilgrimage feast, on the fifteenth day of the seventh month, Tishri. This week long observance marked the end of the grape and olive harvest in the fall of the year with camping out in tents, or booths. In contrast to the Day of Atonement, this was a joyful, festive celebration. People made tents out of palm leaves and willow branches used for joyful processions (2 Maccabees 10:6-8). The Feast of Tabernacles recalled Israel's time of sojourn in the desert. Thanksgiving was offered for the good harvest, and prayers were offered to beg for rain for the coming year. Water from the pool of Siloam was poured around the temple and shaken from myrtle branches.

Jesus used the occasion of the Feast of Tabernacles to teach about the Holy Spirit. "On the last day of the feast, the great day, Jesus stood up and proclaimed, 'If any one thirst, let him come to me and drink. He who believes in me, as the Scripture has said, "Out of his heart shall flow rivers of living water."' Now this he said about the Spirit, which those who believed in him were to receive; for as yet the Spirit had not been given, because Jesus was not yet glorified" (John 7:37–39).

While the feasts and festivals marked special events in the life of the people of God, continuous worship of the Lord was commissioned to the priests. A seven-branch lampstand, the *menorah,* was to burn continually with pure olive oil, in front of the Holy of Holies in the Temple. Twelve freshly baked loaves of bread, perhaps representing the twelve tribes of Israel, were continually offered as the showbread, or bread of the Presence, as prescribed in Exodus 25:30. The showbread was to be eaten by the priests in a holy place.

The Punishment for Blasphemy — The incident of blasphemy recorded in Leviticus 24:10–25, gives the only piece of narrative in this section of scripture. Speaking against the most holy Name of God was punishable by stoning, because it is such a serious offense against God. A man whose father was an Egyptian committed the sin of blasphemy. It was unthinkable that an Israelite would commit such a serious offense against God. The recounting of this incident of blasphemy helps one to understand the seriousness of the accusations later made against Jesus (John 10:33, 19:7). Jesus claimed to be the Son of God. In doing so, He would have to be either telling the truth, in which case He was someone worthy of being worshipped and adored, or else, if lying, a blasphemer, punishable by stoning to death.

Along with sabbath rest and special feasts and festivals throughout the year, there was also provision for the land to have periodic rest. The land was a gift from the Lord. God decreed that, in the seventh year, the land would be left fallow. At that time people could not have known what agricultural science has proven to be a wise practice. Leaving the fields uncultivated at periodic intervals ensures the future fertility of the soil. The Irish Potato Famine of 1845–1849 was the result of a combination of political, biological, and economic problems. However, while an airborne fungus caused the potatoes to rot, the land was also weakened, from planting the same crop on the same land, year after year, without rest.

The Jubilee Year, the year following the seventh sabbatical year, began with the blowing of a ram's horn on the Day of Atonement. Since land was a divine gift from God, the Jubilee Year provided the means for the land to be returned to its rightful owners, to whom the Lord had originally given it. This special blessing allowed those who had fallen upon hard times to regain their family land. In the Catholic Church, the Pope declares a Jubilee Year, in which Christians can receive special graces and indulgences. The Jubilee Year reflects the mercy of God and His concern for the poor and the needy. All people need God's mercy and grace.

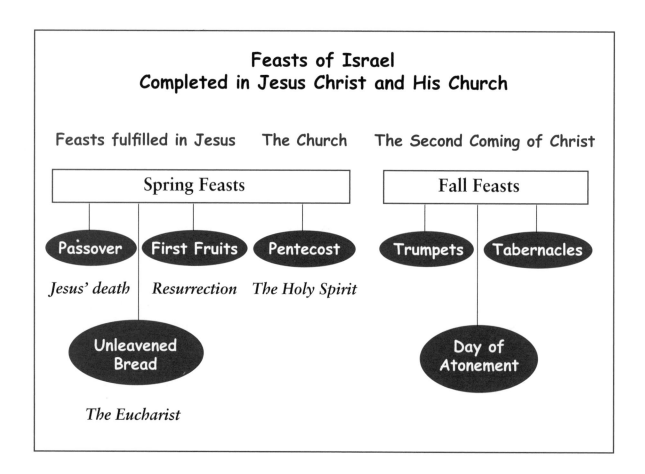

1. What does God command in Leviticus 23:1–3?

2. How can you fulfill the moral command of the sabbath? CCC 2175, 2176

3. Explain the feast described in Leviticus 23:4–8.

4. What does the Passover feast commemorate? Exodus 23:14–17

5. In your own words, describe the Feast of Weeks. Leviticus 23:15–22

6. What specific practice can be found for the feast in Leviticus 23:23–25?

7. What must one do on the Day of Atonement? Leviticus 23:26–32

8. Fill in this chart to describe the Feast of Booths.

Alternate Name	John 7:2
Duration	Leviticus 23:33–38
Preparation	Leviticus 23:39–41
Activity	Leviticus 23:42
Purpose	Leviticus 23:43

9. Find a common theme from following verses.

Leviticus 23:4–15		Mark 14:12–22	
Leviticus 23:10		1 Corinthians 15:23	
Leviticus 23:16		Acts 2:1–4	
Leviticus 23:24		Matthew 24:30–31 1 Corinthians 15:52	
Leviticus 23:28		Romans 5:11	
Leviticus 23:42		Revelation 21:3	

10. What is the punishment decreed for blasphemy? Leviticus 24:16

11. List some examples of continual worship.

Leviticus 24:1–4	
Leviticus 24:5–9	
1 Thessalonians 5:16–18	
Revelation 7:14–17	

12. Describe the sabbatical year from Leviticus 25:1–7.

13. What was the purpose of the Jubilee Year? Leviticus 25:8–34

14. What does God command in Leviticus 25:17?

15. How should one treat a brother who becomes poor? Leviticus 25:35–55

* Have you ever been in a position to help a family member who has fallen upon hard times? Or have you received such help? Share this with your group.

16. Describe some rewards of obedience. Leviticus 26

17. What is the best reward of obedience? Leviticus 26:12

18. List some punishments for disobedience to God. Leviticus 26:14–39

19. Read Leviticus 27 and give a title to the chapter.

20. How could you more faithfully observe the sabbath and holy days?

CHAPTER 14

The Census
Numbers 1–9

The LORD bless you and keep you:
The LORD make his face to shine upon you, and be gracious to you:
The LORD lift up his countenance upon you,
and give you peace.
Numbers 6:24–26

The Book of Numbers gets its name from the Greek translation of the Bible, which focused on the arithmetic of the census account of the people of Israel, covered in the first few chapters of this book. However, the Hebrew name for this book, *Bemidbar*, which means "in the desert," may be a better title, since it describes the plight of the Chosen People wandering in the desert on their way to the Promised Land. After having been rescued from their plight of slavery in Egypt, they now have the freedom to follow God in obedience, or to disobey to their peril.

The section of Sacred Scripture beginning in Exodus 19, and continuing through Numbers 10:11 has been called "The Sinai Pericope." (*Pericope* is a term for a specially selected Bible segment.) God dwells among His people, as He leads them through a desert sojourn, on their way to the Promised Land. This desert experience proves to be a time of trial and testing, but also a time where God establishes an intimate relationship with His people. There are many parallels for each individual who seeks to follow God, and for the people of God as a whole.

For example, each person is a stranger and sojourner on this earth. After leaving behind the slavery of original sin, washed away in baptism, the believer longs for intimacy with God on the way to heaven. More often than not, God uses the desert experiences of life—the trials, temptations, and difficulties to reveal His providence and care. These challenges are often difficult at the time, but remembered with fondness later. Older adults often share with their children the happy times, when they were just starting out, struggling with finances in a tiny home, as the times when they felt closest to God, and most aware of His providence.

God is a God of order. A census precedes the positioning of the men of military age, tribe by tribe, in specific order. The tribe of Judah is the largest. These large numbers fulfill God's promise made to Abraham, to make him a great nation, with descendants like the dust of the earth (Genesis 12:2, 28:14). The twelve tribes of Israel prefigure the twelve apostles, on whom Christ will build His Church.

Only the tribe of Levi, set apart for the Lord's service and ineligible for military combat, is excluded from the census count. God appoints Aaron and his sons as high priests over the men of Levi, all of whom share in the Levitical priesthood. The Levites, as a group, substitute for the firstborn from all twelve tribes. As a reminder of God's sovereignty, the priests and Levites carry out liturgical functions in the manner decreed by God. The people of God respect the choice of God and His specific directives, rather than considering their own personal preferences.

The arrangement of the camp of Israel has theological significance. In the center is the tabernacle, the dwelling of God, and the people are arranged around it. God, the Holy One, dwells in the center of His people, inviting all of His people to make themselves holy and come into His presence. Catholics use the same word "tabernacle" to designate that central sacred place, where Jesus Christ is present, Body, Blood, soul, and divinity, in the Eucharist. The care that the Levites took for the dwelling of God in their midst provides an example for the respect that should be given to the Lord dwelling in our presence in the Blessed Sacrament on the altar.

> For this reason, the real focal point is the *Majestas Domini*, the risen Lord lifted up on high, who is seen at the same time and above all as the one returning, the one already coming in the Eucharist. In the celebration of the liturgy the Church moves toward the Lord; liturgy is virtually this act of approaching his coming. In the liturgy the Lord is already anticipating his promised coming. Liturgy is anticipated Parousia, the "already" entering our "not yet," as John described it in the account of the wedding at Cana. The hour of the Lord has not yet come; all that must happen is not yet fulfilled, but at Mary's—the Church's—request Jesus does give the new wine now and already bestows in advance the gift of his hour.
>
> Pope Benedict XVI, *A New Song for the Lord*
> (New York, NY: Crossroads, 1996), p. 165.

The people of Israel, drawn up in perfect formation around the dwelling of God, foreshadows the new Jerusalem, which was seen by the prophet Ezekiel in a vision (Ezekiel 48:30–35). A similar vision was seen by Saint John, on the island of Patmos, which he described in the book of Revelation (Revelation 21:10–14). And the Gospel of Saint John reveals that "the Word became flesh and dwelt [literally camped, or pitched his tent] among us, full of grace and truth" (John 1:14). From the outset, God was not a distant being, far removed from his people. Rather, God chose to dwell close to His people, in the center of the camp.

When God commands the separate census of the Levites, all males from one month old are counted (Numbers 3:14). The duties and care of liturgical objects is recorded with great precision. The care of the holy things of God requires adherence to God's specific and detailed instructions, according to His good pleasure. It is not for people to decide. This shows the veneration and respect that must be given to the things of God and the preferences of God for worship. Where God is present everything must be clean and pure. Disease, defilement, and sin have no place in the presence of the all-holy, all-pure, all-perfect God. Because God dwells in the camp, every form of sin or uncleanness must be removed.

Later, Jesus Christ would make all things new and would perfect the Law. Jesus welcomed lepers, healed them, and made them clean (Luke 5:12–15; 17:11–15). Jesus, being perfect and truly God, is above defilement. With great compassion, Jesus had no fear of approaching a dead child, touching the body, and restoring her to life (Matthew 9:18–26). Furthermore, Jesus taught that true defilement originates in the evil thoughts and desires of unclean hearts (Matthew 15:18–20). The underlying message is that one must purify oneself to come into the presence of the pure and holy God. Jesus has the power to cleanse and purify everyone.

Moral purity surpasses all natural considerations for cleanliness. Numbers 5 deals very specifically with restitution for sin. Stealing represents a moral offense against God and neighbor. Restitution must be made in full, with an additional gift added on. Likewise cleanliness required that the marriage bed be honored. Marital fidelity was important in the Old Testament as well as the New Testament. Adultery, when proven, was punishable by death for both of the parties (Leviticus 20:10).

Numbers 5:11–31 presents a strategy for a man who suspects his wife of adultery, where there is no proof. The man brings his wife to the priest and accuses her. She is given bitter water to drink. If the bitter water doesn't harm her, she is assumed to be innocent. Oddly, there is no similar prescription for a wife, who suspects her husband of unfaithfulness. Later, Jesus shows a perfect example of mercy. A woman who had been caught in the act of adultery, was brought before Jesus by the scribes and Pharisees. They wanted to see if Jesus would enforce the law and stone the woman to death. Jesus surprised them by asking anyone without sin to cast the first stone. Jesus did not put the woman to death, but He did not ignore her sin, nor make light of it. Jesus says, "Has no one condemned you? ... Neither do I condemn you; go, and do not sin again" (John 8:11).

The Lord explained to Moses a particular type of moral purity in the Nazirite vow (Numbers 6:1–21). A man or woman could choose to make a special vow to the Lord and separate himself or herself for the service of the Lord. Nazirites abstained from strong drink, allowed their hair to grow without cutting, and avoided contact with a dead body. An angel prophesied to Samson's mother, before his birth, that he would take a Nazirite vow (Judges 13:2–7). The same may have been true for Samuel (1 Samuel 1). Nazarites are found in the book of Amos (Amos 2:11) and in the time of Maccabees (1 Maccabees 3:49). Perhaps John the Baptist was a Nazirite, and Saint Paul may have taken a Nazirite vow for a time (Acts 18:18).

Priestly Blessing — One of the earliest priestly blessings in the Bible is found here. "The LORD bless you and keep you: The LORD make his face to shine upon you, and be gracious to you: The LORD lift up his countenance upon you, and give you peace" (Numbers 6:24–26). This triple blessing could anticipate the three persons of the Blessed Trinity. The gifts of love, grace, and peace, come from God the Father, Son, and Holy Spirit. The Roman Missal contains this blessing as one of the texts that a priest may choose for the final blessing at Holy Mass.

God's Presence Infuses Every Aspect of Daily Life. Numbers 7–9 recounts the dedication of the dwelling of God. The rite of consecration reflects the precise directives given by God to the people. The leaders present specific offerings to the Lord on behalf of the whole community. A personal application for the person of this day could be to emulate Israel's submission to God, and their generosity in worship and sacrifice.

The golden lampstand or *menorah,* with seven candles, was an essential feature of divine worship. The ceremony of dedication in Numbers 8:1–23, reveals that the priests were consecrated to the Lord, whereas the Levites were only cleansed. What type of purification of soul, and cleansing of thoughts, should be performed for those coming into the presence of Lord for worship today?

The celebration of the Passover in Sinai was a vital aspect of worship for the Israelites in obedience to the feasts given by God. The Passover enabled them to recall how God had delivered them from the bondage of slavery in Egypt. All of Israel was expected to take part in the Passover celebration. In a similar way, all Catholics are expected to take full and active part in the paschal mystery, which is celebrated in the holy sacrifice of the Mass each Sunday. As the Israelites partook of the Passover lamb, the Catholic consumes the Eucharist, the Lamb of God who takes away the sin of the world.

God Led and Directed His People in the Desert of Sinai. The presence of the Lord was seen in the appearance of fire over the tabernacle at night (Numbers 9:16), and a cloud covering the tabernacle during the day (Numbers 9:15). When the cloud remained over the tabernacle in the camp, the Israelites stayed in the camp. When the cloud set out, the Israelites followed. The cloud shielded the Israelites from the oppressive heat of the sun beating down on them in the desert. God used ordinary visible elements of nature to reveal His divine presence and protection.

The presence of God in a cloud seems to appear in the New Testament as well. When the angel Gabriel appears to the Virgin Mary in Nazareth, asking her to become the mother of the Messiah, she questions how this could come about, since she has no husband. The angel says to Mary, "The Holy Spirit will come upon you, and the power of the Most High will *overshadow* you; therefore the child to be born will be called holy, the Son of God" (Luke 1:35, emphasis added). The Virgin Mary becomes a living tabernacle, holding the Messiah, the Son of God, under her heart in her own body. She is the new Ark of the Covenant, providing a place for God to dwell.

Just as God dwelt in the midst of the people of Israel, God continues to dwell with His Church today. God is present to guide the Church and the people of God through the desert experiences of this life on pilgrimage to the Promised Land. In the contemporary setting, the people of God look to Him in humility to discern the ways in which worship and liturgy should be conducted in a fashion that pleases Almighty God and brings glory and honor to Him.

1. Complete the first census of Israel.

Numbers 1:21	Reuben	46,500
Numbers 1:23		
Numbers 1:25		
Numbers 1:27		
Numbers 1:29		
Numbers 1:31		
Numbers 1:33		
Numbers 1:35		
Numbers 1:37		
Numbers 1:39		
Numbers 1:41		
Numbers 1:43		

2. What was the total number of men? Numbers 1:46

3. Explain the promise fulfilled in the numbers above. Genesis 22:17

4. Where is the tent of meeting positioned? Numbers 2:17

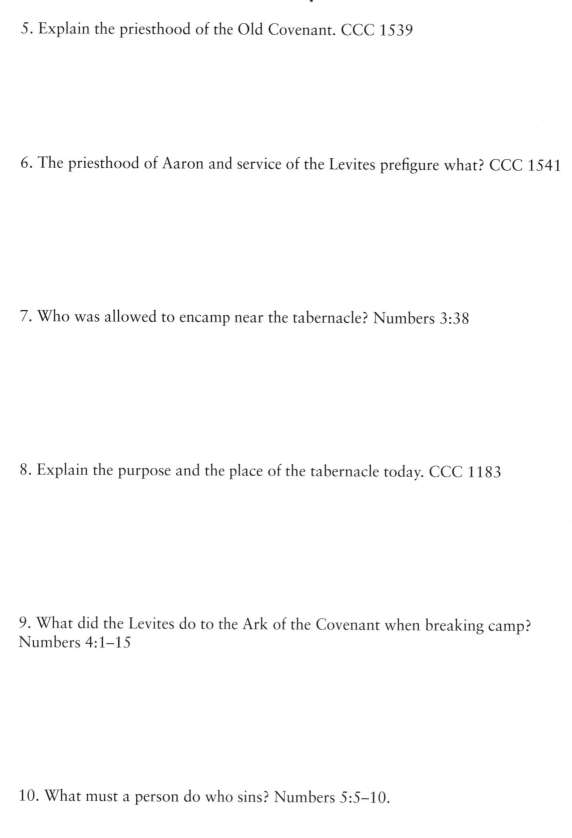

5. Explain the priesthood of the Old Covenant. CCC 1539

6. The priesthood of Aaron and service of the Levites prefigure what? CCC 1541

7. Who was allowed to encamp near the tabernacle? Numbers 3:38

8. Explain the purpose and the place of the tabernacle today. CCC 1183

9. What did the Levites do to the Ark of the Covenant when breaking camp? Numbers 4:1–15

10. What must a person do who sins? Numbers 5:5–10.

11. Explain the scenario in Numbers 5:11–31.

12. List the three components of the Nazirite vow. Numbers 6:1–21.

13. Identify some probable Nazirites from the passages below.

Judges 13	
1 Samuel 1–2	
Luke 1:13–17	

14. Write the blessing found in Numbers 6:24–26.

* Devise a contemporary way in which you could give a blessing to someone.

15. What did Moses do in Numbers 7:89?

16. How often did the high priest invoke the name of God? Where? CCC 433

17. How were the Levites cleansed for the service of the Lord? Numbers 8:5–25

18. Describe the feast held in Sinai. Numbers 9:1–14

19. How did God lead His people in the desert? Numbers 9:15–23

20. How can God lead you through the desert experiences of your life? John 16:13, Revelation 3:20

** If you do not feel that the Holy Spirit is leading you in your life, invite Jesus to come into your heart right now and ask the Holy Spirit to lead you every day.

CHAPTER 15

Into the Desert
Numbers 10, 12–21

**If there is a prophet among you, I the Lord make myself known to him in a vision,
I speak with him in a dream.
Not so with my servant Moses; he is entrusted with all my house.
With him I speak mouth to mouth, clearly, and not in dark speech;
and he beholds the form of the Lord**
Numbers 12:6–8

The desert, with its arid land, characterized by intense heat during the day and bitter cold at night, requires preparedness, discipline, and respect for the demands of nature. Failing to bring food, water, and cover, one cannot survive the harsh elements. The desert is a place of trial and testing for the Chosen People. Had they been obedient to God and expressed gratitude for their deliverance from slavery, perhaps they could have gone directly into the Promised Land. However, because of their disobedience to the Lord and their nostalgia for their old ways in Egypt, Israel must wander in the desert for forty years before entering into the land of the promise. While the desert is a place of trials and temptations, the desert can also provide an opportunity to grow in intimacy with God.

The Catholic Church recalls the forty years of wandering in the desert in the yearly forty-day observance of Lent. Beginning with Ash Wednesday, the Church invites the faithful to enter into a time of voluntary self–denial, fasting, almsgiving, penitential practices, and spiritual exercises in an effort to grow in holiness and draw closer to God. Retreats and pilgrimages may also offer an opportunity to withdraw from the regular activities of daily life to seek out the divine will of God.

Departure from Sinai — The Israelites remained at the foot of Mount Sinai for almost a year before setting out, at God's initiative by the movement of the cloud, toward the wilderness to the south. The Lord guides the people en route in a good order, a liturgical procession, in contrast to the disorder of their rebellion. The Levites are responsible for the tabernacle and are divided into two groups. Because of the arrangement of the Levites, those who carry the Ark of the Covenant will find that the tent of meeting is already set up when the Ark arrives.

Sadly, the wandering in the desert becomes the setting for more disobedience and rebellion of the people of Israel (Numbers 11, 13–14), the Levites (Numbers 16), and even Moses and Aaron (Numbers 20). Despite the weakness and failings of the Lord's people and the Lord's anointed, God remains faithful.

Following the grumbling of the people concerning their hunger and longing for the foods of Egypt, Miriam and Aaron complain against Moses. Jealousy seems to be the motivation for Miriam and Aaron's attempt to grasp more power. Miriam's complaint against her brother Moses results in a severe punishment. And while both Miriam and Aaron are guilty of wrongdoing, only Miriam is stricken with leprosy. Aaron acknowledges his sin to Moses: "Oh, my lord, do not punish us because we have done foolishly and have sinned" (Numbers 12:11). Brashly, Miriam and Aaron demand equal authority with Moses. By failing to accept God's freedom to assign roles and charisms in the way He chooses, to whomever He chooses, these dissenters prefer their own human logic over God's divine wisdom. The severity of Miriam's punishment, and the speed of her complete cure after Moses' prayer, proves that God's anointing rests in a profound way upon Moses. Indeed, Moses is greater than the prophets, because God speaks directly to Moses, not in dreams or visions as with the prophets.

It should be pointed out for those who live in a society fixated on "rights" that no one has a "right" to any position of authority in God's plan. God is sovereign. God chooses whomever He wills for the tasks and responsibilities He assigns. Miriam was a prophetess in her own right. She had been given gifts by God and led the people in singing and dancing when they had been delivered from their slavery in Egypt. But Miriam was not content. She wanted more. Indeed, she demanded more. The self-assertiveness of Miriam is contrasted by the meekness of her brother Moses. Humility is clearly the virtue that God prefers and honors.

The Reconnaissance of Canaan — God directed Moses to send scouts from each of the tribes of Israel to reconnoiter the land of Canaan. Joshua, whose name means "Yahweh saves," and Caleb came back with a positive report, advising Moses to go up and seize the land. However, the majority of the spies gave a negative report, based on fear of the inhabitants. This passage shows that a majority opinion can often be wrong. In England, in the 1500s, most bishops followed the directives of Henry VIII and married. One bishop of a poor, small area, Rochester, refused to follow the majority and remained obedient to the Bishop of Rome. Can you name any of the bishops in the majority? The Bishop of Rochester, imprisoned and beheaded on June 22, 1535, is Saint John Fisher.

After giving in to fear and refusing to enter the Promised Land on God's order, the people plan to replace Moses with someone more to their liking and return to Egypt. Aaron stands with Moses, and Joshua and Caleb stand together in unity. Realizing that they have missed a divine opportunity, the people now fall into the sin of presumption. Refusing to seize the Promised Land on God's strength, they presume to seize Canaan by their own might, which leads predictably to disaster. The problem in both instances is that the people have forgotten to rely totally on God. Rather than following God's commands and walking in His perfect will, the people substitute human plans and worldly logic for God's plan and divine wisdom, which is always in the best interest of humankind.

The early Church Fathers saw the Promised Land as a pre-figuration of heaven. The only way to get to heaven is by following God's plan and invitation. Some people refuse to believe and choose a different plan, which seems more suitable to their own personal preferences. However, those who don't want to be excluded from the celestial banquet in the Promised Land of eternity, accept the invitation of God quickly and obey God's Word completely.

Worship and Sacrifice — While God calls all people to be holy, and all people are to worship Him, only priests are authorized by God to approach the dwelling, to come into the presence of God, the All–holy One and to present offerings which are acceptable to Him. Once again, God's choice is sovereign. While each person, created in the image and likeness of God, is called to be holy, each must be holy in the vocation that God gives. Each person must be faithful to his or her particular state in life. Ambition for power, or a desire for recognition, can motivate people to demand the right to a position, which God has not assigned. Rebellion against the order established by God leads inevitably to disastrous consequences. No one should use religion to attempt to manipulate God for one's own advantage.

The Rebellion of Korah — God responds decisively to rebellion. Korah and his followers were Levites, and already held a prominent place in the nation of Israel. Moses is shocked that being singled out for the Lord's service from the community of Israel is not enough for them. They want more. Indeed, they demand more. They want the place of prominence. They want to be like Moses and Aaron.

Moses, in his characteristic humility, falls prostrate before the Lord. His posture indicates that God is sovereign. Moses worships God and acknowledges his dependence upon God. God can forgive. God can judge the hearts of people. God is God. He determines what is right and fitting. He determines what is just. Moses directs the two hundred fifty followers of Korah to bring censors before the Lord. The Lord judges by sending fire to consume the rebellious Levites of Korah.

The people blame the deaths of the two hundred fifty followers of Korah on Moses and Aaron. The glory of the Lord appears and God's anger is displayed. God tells Moses and Aaron to step back so that He can destroy the entire people! Moses acts swiftly to assuage God's anger, as the people were already falling. Fourteen thousand seven hundred people died from this scourge.

God decides to put an end to the grumbling of the people by revealing His choice in the midst of the people. God tells Moses to get one staff from each tribe of Israel and to mark each man's name on his staff. Aaron's name was marked on the staff for the tribe of Levi. Each staff was laid down in the tent of meeting in front of the commandments. The following day, Aaron's staff had sprouted shoots and blossoms and even ripe almonds. The staff of Aaron clearly showed God's choice and election. In a similar way, the Church has depicted Saint Joseph with a flowering staff to show his selection as the one God chose to care for His Son.

God Directs in a Clear and Specific Fashion. Only a priest may approach the altar. God assigns those who may perform priestly functions. The people pay tithes to support the priests and Levites. God is teaching His people about His very nature, the holiness and transcendent nature of God. Profaning the sacred gifts for the Lord will bring a disastrous result, even death to the arrogant.

A perfect red heifer, free from blemish or defect, was to be sacrificed by the priest outside of the camp. Saint Cyril of Alexandria saw the red heifer as a prefigurement of Jesus Christ, the One without sin or defect, who was immolated so that we might live. The water for purification prefigures the waters of baptism, which cleanse each person from the effects of original sin.

Regulations concerning contact with a dead body reflect God's instruction on the importance of everything having to do with life and death. God is the Author and Giver of life. God alone gives life, and in death the soul returns to God for judgment. The sanctity of human life is already revealed in the Sacred Scriptures of antiquity. People show respect for the human body, and carefully purify themselves after contact with a dead body before returning to the community.

More Trials in the Desert — Miriam dies in the desert of Zin. The lack of water in the desert causes the people to grumble once again. Once again, Moses and Aaron prostrate themselves before the Lord to beg His mercy. God gives Moses and Aaron instructions, and sadly even Moses and Aaron sin grievously before the Lord. To the sin of the people is now added the sin of the leaders. The exact nature of the sin of Moses and Aaron is unclear. One possibility is that Moses and Aaron were instructed to speak to the rock, or to strike it once, and instead struck it twice. Another possibility is that Moses spoke "rash words," so that Moses' speech or anger may have been the problem. Or perhaps, Moses and Aaron failed to give God the credit for providing the water and implied that they had power apart from God to do signs and wonders. Whatever the specific sin may have been, Moses and Aaron will not enter the Promised Land as punishment.

Despite the sins of the people, and the sins of the leaders, God still fulfills the promises He made to His people. Sin does not have the power to annul God's promise. God fulfills His divine plan for His chosen people, even though they are weak and often unfaithful. God is always faithful.

Once again the people grumble and complain, and serpents bite the people so that many of them die. When Moses prays for the people, God directs him to make a bronze serpent on a pole. Whenever anyone who was bitten by a snake looked at the bronze serpent he recovered. Saint John used this imagery to show Jesus being lifted up on the Cross to save sinners. The Catholic Church offers readings from Numbers 21:4–9 along with John 8:21–30 in the Liturgy of the Word on Tuesday of the fifth week of Lent. On the threshold of the Promised Land, the people and leaders are tempted to forget God and resort to human logic and reasoning. Moses clearly shows that God is sovereign. Moses was meek and humble. He frequently prostrated himself before a merciful and loving God. A man or woman today would be wise to be humble, prayerful, and obedient to God.

1. What prayer did Moses pray whenever the Ark set out? Numbers 10:35

2. Explain the drama in Numbers 12 in your own words.

Numbers 12:1–8	
Numbers 12:9–12	
Numbers 12:13–16	

3. What did the majority of spies report to Moses and Aaron? Numbers 13:25–29

4. Caleb gave what recommendation? Numbers 13:30–33

5. How does Moses pray for the people? CCC 2577

6. Explain the sequence of events in your own words.

Numbers 14:1–4	
Numbers 14:5–10	
Numbers 14:11–12	
Numbers 14:13–19	
Numbers 14:20–38	
Numbers 14:39–45	

7. Who may make a sin offering for the people to the Lord? Numbers 15:25

8. Why does the Lord prescribe tassels on clothes? Numbers 15:37–41

9. Explain Korah's and Moses' positions. Numbers 16:1–11

10. What happened to Dathan and Abiram? Numbers 16:12–34

11. Describe what happened to Aaron's staff. Numbers 17

12. What can you learn from the following passages?

Numbers 18	
CCC 1540	
CCC 1542	

13. How does the New Testament passage explain the situation in Numbers 19?

Numbers 19	
Hebrews 9:13–15	

14. What sad event happened at the beginning of Numbers 20?

15. Compare the following passages.

Numbers 20:2–11	
1 Corinthians 10:1–4	

16. What do you think Moses and Aaron did wrong? Numbers 20

17. Describe the problem in Numbers 21:4–5.

18. What punishment ensued? Numbers 21:6–7

19. Compare the following passages.

Numbers 21:4–9	
John 3:14; 8:21–30	

20. What can God do in the desert? Hosea 2:14–15 RSVCE, Hosea 2:16–17 NAB

* Have you ever gone on retreat or to adoration of the Blessed Sacrament to listen to the Lord speak to you personally? Share the results with your small group.

CHAPTER 16

Discipline
Numbers 22-36

**I see him, but not now; I behold him, but not nigh:
a star shall come forth out of Jacob,
and a scepter shall rise out of Israel;**
Numbers 24:17

Israel on the Plains of Moab — From this point in the narrative of the Book of Numbers until the end of the Book of Deuteronomy, Israel remains on the plains of Moab, before the city of Jericho, at the gateway to the Promised Land. While detailed preparations are being made for the Chosen People to cross the River Jordon into the Promised Land, Israel falls once again into grievous sin. The grave sin of idolatry results in severe punishment.

The Oracles of Balaam — An interesting drama is recorded in Numbers 22–24, as Balak, the king of Moab, fearing the strength of Israel, calls on Balaam to curse Israel for him. Balaam is a seer or soothsayer from Mesopotamia. Despite the fact that Balaam is not an Israelite, he is aware of the God of Israel and respectful of Him. He listens to God and tells Balak that he can only speak what the Lord gives him to say. He is not a prophet for hire, but heeds God. Initially Balaam refuses to go with the servants of Balak, but later he acquiesces.

In Numbers 22:28–30, a dumb animal, Balaam's ass, speaks. This may be reminiscent of the passages in Genesis 3:1–5 when a reptile, the serpent, speaks to Eve. In this passage, the seer Balaam stubbornly fails to recognize the signs of God, while a dumb animal clearly sees the angel of the Lord blocking his path. Perhaps the lesson for us is to be docile to the subtle warnings that God sends. Saint Augustine saw in this passage an example of God "choosing the least in this world to confound the wise." This passage should be a warning to those who fall easily into the sin of pride, believing that they know clearly the will of God, while stubbornly refusing to see the warnings that God places directly in front of them.

Balaam's four oracles praise the nation of Israel, highlighting God's election of a people to be His own, set apart from other nations. It is not a prophet of Israel who pronounces these four oracles. Rather, a foreigner proclaims God's blessing upon Israel! Balaam is given a vision of the future glory and splendor of Israel. Balaam sees a star, which shall come forth out of Jacob (Numbers 24:17). The early Church Fathers saw the star in Balaam's vision as the same star the Magi saw in Bethlehem (Matthew 2:1–12). Balaam came from Mesopotamia, and the Wise Men were also from Mesopotamia. The greatest splendor to come from the nation of Israel was the Child wrapped in swaddling clothes, lying under the star of Bethlehem, which the Magi pursued and found with great joy.

Idolatrous Israel — God is the one true God and deserves undivided love from the people He has chosen and delivered from slavery. Israel sinned through lack of faith, disobedience, and grumbling against God and His anointed. Now, Israel falls into an even more serious sin, that of idolatry. The Chosen People prostitute themselves both in a physical and a spiritual sense. First, they commit the sin of fornication with foreign women. Secondly, they worship foreign idols. God warned the people in the very first commandment that He would not tolerate the worship of other gods. The challenge for Israel and the challenge facing Christians today, involves remaining faithful to the one true God while living in the midst of a pagan culture. The believer must learn to remain faithful to God, while interacting with people in the world, without being influenced by the sinfulness of the world.

Israel's idolatry so offends the Almighty that twenty-four thousand people die. The priestly duty of restoring the purity of Israel by eliminating the apostasy from the community is extremely severe. Conversely, the laxity in dealing with serious sexual sin in contemporary culture has brought about horrible suffering as well. Phinehas demonstrates his zeal for the Lord, which propels him into destroying the idolaters. God's anger is assuaged and the bloodshed stops.

Census of a New Generation — The census of the old generation was 603,550 people excluding the Levites, according to Numbers 1:46. Most of the old generation that left Egypt have died by this time, with the exception of Caleb and Joshua, who will be permitted to enter the Promised Land with the new generation. The census of the new generation is smaller than the old generation at 601,730 (Numbers 26:51). The numbers of the new census prove that God has kept His promise to Israel. Despite their sin and infidelity, God remains faithful and true to His word.

Because of his sin, Moses will die before entering the Promised Land. But, unlike his brother Aaron, Moses is allowed to see the Promised Land from a distance before he dies. Moses will not leave the people without a leader, but assigns Joshua to lead the people across the Jordan to the land of promise. Joshua has already demonstrated his leadership abilities, and now Moses will lay hands on Joshua to impart his blessing and authority. While Joshua will lead the people, he will not receive all of the spirit and authority that belonged to Moses, for Moses was unique. He alone spoke face to face with God.

Inheritance Rights of Daughters — God promised Abraham land and descendants. The land is a gift from God that is carefully apportioned according to the tribes of Israel. Because the land is a gift from God, apportioned according to His will, every precaution is taken to keep the land within the respective families and tribes. In the case where there is no male heir to inherit the land, a provision is made for female heirs to retain the family land (Numbers 27:1–11). Later, in Numbers 36 the heiresses are directed by Moses to marry within their own family tribe because, should they marry outside the tribe, their family land would be lost to another tribe. The daughters of Zelophehad, who had no brothers, obeyed the command, which the Lord had given through Moses, and married within their tribe.

Liturgical Feasts and Sacrifices — Numbers 28–29 specifies liturgical feasts and offerings for the Chosen People. Sacrifices are taken from the goods of creation, both from agriculture and livestock, to be offered back to God. Everything comes from God, and the first and the best should be returned to Him in thanksgiving. These feasts and sacrifices will keep the Lord in the forefront of the minds and hearts of the people of Israel. Although many of the feasts have been discussed in detail earlier, the new generation going into the Promised Land must clearly understand the feasts of the Lord, in order to demonstrate their faithfulness to God and offer Him the worship that is His due.

These offerings actually give nothing to God, since it was all His at the outset. Nevertheless, it keeps God in the minds of His people. It was essential for Moses to teach the people the importance of offering a sacrifice to God, as His due. In contemporary society, it is also important to impress upon believers that worship is something that is given to God, because it is His due, not because someone feels like it, is entertained, or gets something out of it. The Christian worships God to offer a sacrifice of praise to God and, in return, is given grace from God. The attitude of the believer reflects that worship and sacrifice are an obligation given to an all-holy God by a person who has nothing to give that has not been given to him. The only thing that can be given to God is love, obedience, and worship.

The Validity and Annulment of Vows — A vow is a solemn promise made to God. One type of vow would be the voluntary promise of lifelong virginity to God. In this case, a person would consecrate his or her entire life to God alone. Yet family order and responsibility remain of critical importance. An unmarried woman would be under the authority of her father. If her father opposes her vow, then the Lord will release her from her solemn promise. However, if her father says nothing in opposition to her, then the vow of the unmarried woman is binding before God.

Marriages were made differently in ancient Hebrew culture, than in contemporary culture. Commonly, a marriage would be arranged by the father of a young man and the father of a young woman. A bride price was paid and gifts of land and livestock were given. The prospective bride and groom might not even meet before the wedding. If on the wedding day, a woman's husband learns of her vow and disapproves of it, the Lord will release her from her vow. But, if her husband says nothing, then her vow will stand. Tradition reveals that the Blessed Virgin Mary made a vow of perpetual virginity from her youth. Clearly Saint Joseph became aware of Mary's vow of virginity, honored it, and preserved it.

Hebrew culture took vows very seriously. One's word was binding before God. Contemporary society has lost the appreciation of the sacredness of a solemn promise before God. Marriage vows have been taken so lightly that, in some cases, a pre-nuptial agreement specifying the terms of divorce is signed before the wedding. And when one vow is broken, it becomes easier for subsequent promises to become trite and meaningless. The importance of honoring one's word and keeping vows and promises adds stability to a society.

Widows and divorced women are responsible for the fulfillment of their vows in the same way that men are responsible for the fulfillment of their vows according to Mosaic law. Here, women can make vows before God, and are expected to keep their sacred promises. There is no family order to disrupt. Vows of poverty, chastity, and obedience set a person apart entirely for God. Certain vows of fasting and specific penitential practices may also be offered as a sacrifice to God.

The destruction of the Midianites (Numbers 31) occurs to rid the people of Israel of a repeated temptation to sin. Throughout the history of the Chosen People, the danger of idolatry came from the pagan people surrounding them. Israel repeatedly faced the challenge of remaining faithful to God's commands when they intermingled with foreign people with their evil practices. In the New Testament, Jesus will teach that the enemy is sin. People must carefully avoid the works of the world, the flesh, and the devil. Jesus demonstrated how to live a holy life in the midst of unbelievers. Jesus never gave in to temptation or to violence. Jesus showed how to love one's enemies and to pray for persecutors. Jesus was able to live in the midst of evil, yet remain pure and undefiled.

Stages on the Journey — Here on the plains of Moab Israel recalls the stages on the journey through the desert on the way to the Promised Land. God led the people through the wilderness experience, with Moses as their guide and leader. The wandering through the wilderness proves to be an important folk memory for the people to retain and pass on to their children. The hard times of testing will be an important remembrance. So too, in families, often parents will relate to the children and grandchildren the stories of difficult times in order to strengthen the family unity and identity. Families tell stories of immigration to a new land, the newlywed adjustments, the times of financial difficulties, job loss, or serious illnesses. This recollection serves to identify the presence of God through the difficult times and into the joyful times. And in hindsight, many people recall that God seemed closest to them in the difficult desert experiences.

Over the forty years of wandering in the desert, Israel recounted forty-two stops along the way. Some of the early Church Fathers saw the desert experience in light of the Christian's stopping points along the way to heaven. Saint Ambrose saw the forty years in the desert prefiguring the forty days of Lent, preparing to celebrate the Resurrection of Our Lord. Saint Jerome identified the many virtues necessary for Christians's to attain on the way to heaven.

For the people of Israel, their safety and security were assured as they waited on God and followed the leadership of Moses. God was faithful throughout the forty years of wandering. The people always had food and water. Their shoes and clothes never wore out along the way. God provided for every need in each situation. The Christian must also learn to wait on God and to follow the appointed leaders, the priest and bishop. In faithful obedience, the Christian can hope to weather the difficult times with God's help, and at the end of one's days to enter into the Promised Land—eternal joy with God and His saints in heaven.

1. Explain the summoning of Balaam. Numbers 22:1–21

2. Why was God's anger aroused against Balaam?

Numbers 22:22	
2 Peter 2:15–16	
Jude 11	

3. Identify four speakers, and their comments in the following passages.

Numbers 22:28, 30		*What have I done that you struck me?* *Am I not your faithful beast,* *whom you have ridden all your life?*
Numbers 22:32–33 Numbers 22:35		
Numbers 22:29 Numbers 22:34, 38	*Balaam*	
Numbers 22:37		

4. In your own words, describe the four oracles of Balaam.

Numbers 23:7–11	
Numbers 23:18–24	
Numbers 24:1–9	
Numbers 24:14–25	

5. Identify two serious sins Israel committed.

Numbers 25:1	
Numbers 25:2	

6. How was the Lord's anger assuaged? Numbers 25:5–18

7. How was the land apportioned? Numbers 26:52–56

8. Explain the laws concerning heiresses who have no brothers. Numbers 27:1–11

9. What did the Lord tell Moses? Numbers 27:12–14

10. Describe the drama in the following passages.

Numbers 27:15–17	
Numbers 27:18–21	
Numbers 27:22–23	

11. Explain the offerings for various occasions described in Numbers 28.

Numbers 28:1–8	
Numbers 28:9–10	
Numbers 28:11–15	
Numbers 28:16–25	
Numbers 28:26–31	

12. Identify three feasts recounted in Numbers 29.

Numbers 29:1–6	
Numbers 29:7–11	
Numbers 29:12–39	

13. How must a man discharge a vow to the Lord? Numbers 30:1–2 (30:3 NAB)

* Have you ever made a vow to the Lord? If you are married, you have!

14. What happens when a woman takes a vow? Numbers 30:3–17

Unmarried	
Married	
Widowed or Divorced	

15. Briefly explain the drama in Numbers 31.

16. How did Moses solve the dilemma in Numbers 32?

17. What would result if Israel allowed the pagans to remain? Numbers 33:55–56

18. What happens when a family or a community allow a little bit of evil to slip in?

19. Explain the punishments for murder and manslaughter. Numbers 35:16–34

20. What restrictions are placed on the property of heiresses? Numbers 36:1–10

Monthly Social Activity

This month, your small group will meet for coffee, tea, or a simple breakfast, lunch, or dessert in someone's home. Pray for this social event and for the host or hostess. Try, if at all possible, to attend.

After a short prayer and some time for small talk, describe the journey in your spiritual life so far. Try to do this in less than five minutes, so every one will have a chance.

Examples:

◆ *The first stage in my faith journey occurred when I was born into a faith-filled family, and my parents had me baptized as an infant.*

◆ *At my First Holy Communion, I had a deep encounter with the person of Jesus.*

◆ *After drifting away from my faith somewhat in college, I started to pray for a good spouse.*

◆ *With the miracle of the birth of our first child, I came to appreciate the providence of God in a new way. We wanted to raise our children in the Lord, and decided to start to get serious about learning more and practicing our faith.*

CHAPTER 17

The Heart of the Torah
Deuteronomy 1–6

Hear, O Israel: The Lord our God is one Lord;
and you shall love the Lord your God with all your heart,
and with all your soul, and with all your might.
And these words which I command you this day shall be upon your heart;
and you shall teach them diligently to your children,
and shall talk of them when you sit in your house, and when you walk by the
way, and when you lie down, and when you rise.
Deuteronomy 6:4–7

The Heart of the Torah — As discussed in the Introduction, the first five books of the Bible form a group called "Torah," or "The Books of Moses," or "The Pentateuch" (which in Greek means "The Five Scrolls"). These books together form a unity, encapsulating the revelation of Moses, through whom God gave His instructions, the Torah. Though containing many laws and commandments, the term Torah refers to the entire Mosaic code, and also to the entire series of five books, which contain it. There are five books but one Torah, Ten Commandments but one Torah, hundreds of specific pieces of legislation but only one Torah.

"These are the words that Moses spoke" (Deuteronomy 1:1). For the five books of Moses, the Hebrews used the opening phrase as the title, which was left showing when the scroll was rolled up and put on the shelf. The title of the fifth book in Hebrew is "These Are the Words" or simply "Words." The Greeks, on the other hand, assigned to each book a title descriptive of its content, and to the fifth book they gave the name "Deuteronomy" which means "Second Law." The book contains some new legislation, but also recounts the basic law of the Book of Exodus.

The Hebrew and Greek names of all five books are as follows:

IN HEBREW	IN GREEK
Bereshith (In the Beginning)	*Genesis* (Creation)
Shmoth (The Names)	*Exodos* (Departure)
Wayiqre (He Called)	*Leviticos* (Levitical Concerns)
Bammidbar (In the Desert)	*Arithmoi* (Numbers)
Debarim (The Words)	*Deuteronomos* (Second Law)

"In the fortieth year" (Deuteronomy 1:3) — As the fifth "Book of Moses" begins, the Israelites are completing their forty years of wandering in the desert. During this time, they have sought to put into practice the teachings, which they received on Mount Sinai. By now, the spirit of those teachings has become clearer to them, and the Book of Deuteronomy reinterprets those received teachings in the light of subsequent experience. The Israelites have known moral growth as a result of faithfulness to the Torah, and Moses takes this last opportunity, by virtue of his teaching office, to instill an even deeper understanding of the heart of the Torah.

The first several chapters of the book recount the interactions that the Hebrews have had with the peoples of the Sinai region, during the course of their wanderings. The narrative seems at first glance to be yet another collection of sacred war stories. In a land of scarce resources, some conflict with the local population was inevitable as the large body of refugees passed through. The other peoples did not enjoy the gift of manna to sustain them, and feared starvation for themselves and their children. There was only so much water to go around. Some of those who feared for their safety because of the Hebrews became threats to the survival of the Hebrews.

A closer reading shows that the narrator takes care to mention all the tribes with whom the Hebrews have enjoyed peaceful relations. Just as the sea had parted to allow them to pass through dry shod, so for the most part the peoples parted to allow them free passage. The desert tradition of hospitality largely prevailed. A principal factor is that several of the tribes in the area are related to them, and the kinship of blood provides an automatic passport through the countryside.

This narrative shift from conflict to peaceful interaction seems to indicate that the Hebrews became less warlike as they continued wandering. At first their fear level was high, and so they perceived threats all around them to which they responded militarily. Eventually, they learned the lay of the land.

And, in the course of two generations, they gradually became people of the desert themselves. They knew where force was really necessary, and did not apply it any more than necessary. The new commandment "Thou shall not kill" had been slowly working on them, so that the military option became the course of last rather than of first resort. They learned the meaning of the commandment. Jesus caps this development when He instructs Peter, "All who take the sword will perish by the sword" (Matthew 26:52).

"Observe the sabbath day" (Deuteronomy 5:12). For most of the Ten Commandments, Deuteronomy simply repeats the words of Exodus. The shortest commandments read the same way in both accounts: "You shall not kill. You shall not commit adultery. You shall not steal. You shall not bear false witness against your neighbor" (Exodus 20:13-16 and Deuteronomy 5:20).

Some of the longer commandments have explanations attached to them, as in the Second Commandment: "You shall not take the name of the Lord your God in vain; for the Lord will not hold him guiltless who takes his name in vain" (Exodus 20:7 and Deuteronomy 5:11). In the case of that commandment, the explanations are the same, but the Third Commandment finds a whole new rationale in the Deuteronomic account:

Remember the sabbath day, to keep it holy. Six days you shall labor, and do all your work; but the seventh day is a sabbath to the Lord your God; in it you shall not do any work, you, or your son, or your daughter, your manservant, or your maidservant, or your cattle, or the sojourner who is within your gates; for in six days the Lord made heaven and earth, the sea, and all that is in them, and rested the seventh day; therefore the Lord your God has blessed the sabbath day and hallowed it. Exodus 20:8–11	Observe the sabbath day, to keep it holy, as the Lord your God commanded you. Six days you shall labor, and do all your work; but the seventh day is a sabbath to the Lord your God; in it you shall not do any work, you, or your son, or your daughter, or your manservant, or your maidservant, or your ox, or your ass, or any of the cattle, or the sojourner who is within your gates, that your manservant and your maidservant may rest as well as you. You shall remember that you were a servant in the land of Egypt, and the Lord your God brought you out thence with a mighty hand and an outstretched arm; therefore the Lord your God commanded you to keep the sabbath day. Deuteronomy 5:12–15

Exodus mentions the male and female slaves among those who must rest on the sabbath. Although Exodus accommodates itself to the institution of slavery, in effect slavery is abolished one day out of each week. No Hebrew master may tell any slave, Hebrew or foreign, to do work of any kind on the sabbath day. If fire may not be lit, the slave may not be forced to light it either. So sabbath rest is already liberating and equalizing. On the seventh day, the Hebrew king must rest from his labor, along with his courtiers, generals, guards, soldiers, citizens, and slaves of the land.

Deuteronomy takes this one step further. Of the entire list of those who must rest, the menservants and maidservants are singled out for special emphasis. Only they are mentioned a second time. No doubt, during the forty intervening years, the Hebrews had many discussions about slavery, and many of them saw the disparity between their own liberation from Egypt and the continued practice of slavery among them. The implementary legislation of Exodus bent over backwards to accommodate the requirements of the slave masters, but none of that finds any place in the legislation of Deuteronomy. The moral conscience of the people has experienced growth, and while they have not positively abolished slavery, they no longer afford it the privilege of the law. Already in Exodus the institution of the sabbath challenged the absolute supremacy of the slave owner, and in Deuteronomy the tone becomes even more abolitionist.

Something similar happened in American history. George Washington and Thomas Jefferson owned slaves, and were unable to apply their lofty principles of human freedom to their slaves. Eventually their failure caused a great conflict between the states, and Abraham Lincoln demonstrated clear moral superiority over his predecessors in the presidency. Modern people feel repugnant at the idea of one human being owning another. Over time, the values of freedom have settled into the moral fiber of the people. This moral growth began in the desert of Sinai and shows itself in the subtle differences of legal interpretation between Exodus and Deuteronomy.

"Neither shall you covet your neighbor's wife" (Deuteronomy 5:21). The last two commandments also show some substantial growth in interpretation during the forty years between Exodus and Deuteronomy. The status of women has improved. Exodus seems to treat them like chattel, but Deuteronomy accords them the dignity of personhood.

You shall not covet your neighbor's house; you shall not covet your neighbor's wife, or his manservant, or his maidservant, or his ox, or his ass, or anything that is your neighbor's. Exodus 20:17	Neither shall you covet your neighbor's wife; and you shall not desire your neighbor's house, his field, or his manservant, or his maidservant, his ox, or his ass, or anything that is your neighbor's. Deuteronomy 5:21

The legislation in Exodus lists the wife along with other domestic possessions. First comes the house, then what it contains, the wife, the slaves, the animals, and all the sundry property. Deuteronomy recognizes the wife as holding a special place, and so she receives special mention before the house as well as the goods. Recognizing its superiority, the Church has selected the Deuteronomic formula for use in catechesis. So Catholics have learned that the Ninth Commandment is "Thou shall not covet thy neighbor's wife" and the Tenth is "Thou shall not covet thy neighbor's goods." That is the order of Deuteronomy, not of Exodus.

Coveting is defiantly disordered. God gave someone else a wife. If I reject God's will for that husband and desire that wife for myself, I demonstrate that I value the woman more than I value the God who gave her to someone else. That woman becomes my god then, and I try to make myself her god, replacing the God who created each of us. Herein lies a formula for disaster in relationships.

The Ninth Commandment gets to the heart of the Sixth. One should not commit adultery, and should keep a pure heart untainted by lust. Similarly the Tenth Commandment gets to the heart of the Seventh. One should not steal, and should keep a heart unstained by envy. Purity of heart lays the foundation for good behavior. Corruption of heart is the basis for bad actions of all kinds. One should pursue purity of heart both for its own sake and for the benefit of making easier the life of virtue. The Ninth and Tenth Commandments deliver us nearly all the way to the values of the Gospel: "For where your treasure is, there will your heart be also" (Matthew 6:21).

"Love the Lord thy God with all thy heart" (Deuteronomy 6:4). In the time of Jesus the rabbis debated which was the greatest commandment of the Torah, and all parties settled on the passage *Shema Yisrael,* translated "Hear, O Israel" (Deuteronomy 6:4ff). The First Commandment had already banned idolatrous actions, but the "Great Commandment" interiorizes our response in the context of a worshipful heart.

To the ancient Hebrews, the *Lebab,* or heart, was not the seat of emotion, as we use the word, but the wellspring of motivation. The Hebrew mind needed to discover the inner coherence of the Torah received from God. That insight arrives in the Book of Deuteronomy. Two great religions, Judaism and Christianity, find their rationale in that inspired logic of love. Without the practice of love, the law is harsh, and justice is cruel. The heart makes its own demands, which are not limited by the requirements of law. The heart of the Torah is the love of the Lord, whose every wish should be our command.

> **With my whole heart I seek thee;**
> **let me not wander from thy commandments!**
> Psalm 119:10

The heart of the law is love, which originates in God, who *is* Love. Once a person experiences the unfathomable love of God and tastes the mercy of God, it becomes abundantly clear that God is good, all the time. And everything God does is done in love. Therefore, the heart of the law is God's love. God loves the people He has created for Himself. All the laws of God are designed to bring peace, order, love, and joy into relationships. When a person breaks God's law, disorder, betrayal, and ultimately suffering follows. Therefore, to understand the heart of the law, no better preparation can be considered than to meditate on God's immense love. When someone accepts God's love, the grace is available to embrace God's law. Peace, love, and joy are the results of striving for obedience and submission to God.

1. Describe the drama in Deuteronomy 1:1–18.

2. What did the scouts learn? Deuteronomy 1:19–25

3. List some of Israel's sins against God. Deuteronomy 1:26–46

4. What did God do during the forty years in the desert? Deuteronomy 2:7

5. List the following conquests.

Deuteronomy 2:8–15	
Deuteronomy 2:16–25	
Deuteronomy 2:26–37	
Deuteronomy 3:1–11	

6. What did Moses ask God, and how did God answer? Deuteronomy 3:23–29

7. Why did God give the law? CCC 708

8. Explain some advantages of obedience to God's laws. Deuteronomy 4:1–8

Deuteronomy 4:1a	
Deuteronomy 4:1b	
Deuteronomy 4:6	

9. Give some proofs of God's love. Deuteronomy 4:32–40

10–11. Write the Decalogue (Ten Commandments) from Deuteronomy with verses.

I. I am the Lord your God. … You shall have no other gods before me.	Deuteronomy 5:6–7
II.	
III.	
IV.	
V.	Deuteronomy 5:17

12. Describe the full meaning of the Commandments. CCC 2061

The Commandments take on their full meaning ...	
Man's moral life has all its meaning in and through ...	
The first of the "ten words" recalls that ...	

13. What can you learn about the heart?

Psalm 33:21	
Proverbs 4:23	
Matthew 6:21	
Luke 8:15	
Romans 5:5	
CCC 368	

14. What is man's duty toward God?

Deuteronomy 6:5	
Matthew 22:36–38	
CCC 2083	

15. What should be on your heart? Deuteronomy 6:6

16. What is God's first call and just demand?

Deuteronomy 6:13–14	
CCC 2084	

17. How can man respond appropriately to God? CCC 2096

18. To whom do you have a responsibility to teach God's laws?

Deuteronomy 4:9 b	*make them known to your ...*
Deuteronomy 4:9b	*and your ...*
Deuteronomy 6:7	
Deuteronomy 6:20–25	

19. Why should you obey God's laws? Deuteronomy 6:24–25

20. Brainstorm some practical ways you could teach God's laws to your children, grandchildren, or godchildren. Then, do something concrete and share about it.

CHAPTER 18

Obedience and Blessing
Deuteronomy 7–11

**Do not say in your heart, after the Lᴏʀᴅ your God has thrust them before you,
"It is because of my righteousness
that the Lᴏʀᴅ has brought me in to possess this land";
whereas it is because of the wickedness of these nations
that the Lᴏʀᴅ is driving them out before you.**
Deuteronomy 9:4

Obedience and blessing are related to each other as corresponding responsibilities of the two parties to the covenant. Almighty God commits Himself to bless the Israelites, and the Israelites for their part commit to obey Him. God is bound by His word to bless, and Israel by their word to obey.

During the three millennia since the days of Moses, theologians have debated which comes first, the obedience or the blessing. The text of Deuteronomy indicates that God has future blessings in store for the Israelites if they remain faithful to their part of the covenant, but some have worried that this gives the impression of blessing as payment for services rendered. Catholic theologians point out that God's grace goes before us always, preparing the way for us. The technical term for God's preparatory help is "prevenient grace." A good concrete symbol of that kind of grace is the pillar of cloud by day and the pillar of fire by night that led the Israelites out of Egypt.

Grace cannot be limited to the past, the present, or the future. God's grace comes after, as well as before. He does promise rewards to those who cooperate with His grace and help to build His kingdom. The heavenly reward springs not from His justice, however, but from His infinite mercy. No one can earn heaven, but cooperation with grace makes earth more heavenly and heaven our true destiny.

Since all time is simultaneous to God, the principal party to the covenant, perhaps the blessing and the obedience truly happen in a single instant. At the moment the covenant gets ratified, the mutual obligations become binding on both sides. From that instant, God and Israel are bound to remain faithful to one another, just like a husband and wife are bound to one another from the moment of their vows. Each must be faithful because of what he or she has promised, not as a consequence of the behavior of the other. God could never be capricious, proposing that He would be good only if we were good first. Goodness comes to God naturally, but to us only through His help. God knows that our goodness derives entirely from His.

"You shall therefore be careful to do the commandment, and the statutes, and the ordinances, which I command you this day" (Deuteronomy 7:11). "This day" here refers to the final, definitive pronouncement of the Torah at the end of the forty years of wandering in the desert. Although the parties ratified the covenant at the beginning of the wandering, the specifics take some time to get clarified. At the beginning, there seemed to be many commandments comprising one Torah, but by the time of Deuteronomy the Ten Commandments have consolidated into a single, overarching commandment. Note in the above verse (Deuteronomy 7:11), the word "commandment," *mitzvah*, appears in the singular, not in the plural. This refers back to the *Shema*, "Hear, O Israel," of Deuteronomy 6:4.

The English verb "do" does not faithfully render the Hebrew verb *shamar*, which means to guard, to keep, or to protect. No one can "do the commandment." English speakers have learned to "keep the commandment." Perhaps the best translation is to "safeguard the commandment." The Rabbis speak of "building a fence around the commandment," like a protective rampart.

Where casuists try to see how close to the commandment one can get without breaking it, the Rabbis try to ensure that everyone keep far enough away from it to stay safe. Moral theologians fall into two camps, those who give sinners the benefit of the doubt, and those who give the commandment the benefit of the doubt. Those who love God and are faithful to Him should not fall into the adolescent game of asking "How much can I get away with?" Instead one should keep the spirit as well as the letter of the law. Jesus pointed out that: "The sabbath was made for man, not man for the sabbath" (Mark 2:27). By this statement, Jesus does not abrogate the commandment, but points out the mutuality of benefit that it provides—worship to God, and rest to human beings. He points out that the sabbath is something that we do for each other and for ourselves, and not just for God. We need our obedience more than God does. Through obedience we exercise faith in a practical rather than an abstract way. Too many people make a distinction between faith and obedience. The two are combined in the concept of faithfulness. Obedience is faith in practice.

"Know that man does not live by bread alone, but that man lives by everything that proceeds out of the mouth of the Lord" (Deuteronomy 8:4). After forty days in the desert, Jesus quotes the book, which Moses dictated at the end of his forty years in the desert. Moses failed his test, when he doubted at Massah. Moses flinched for just a second when it was time to strike the rock with his staff, but Jesus remains constant and quotes the verse "You shall not put the Lord your God to the test" (Deuteronomy 6:16, quoted in Matthew 4:7).

Jesus experienced hunger in the desert of Judea, just as Moses felt hunger in the Sinai desert. Moses received manna as a divine gift, whereas Jesus spurns the devil's offer of false manna, and quotes the verse "Man does not live by bread alone" (Deuteronomy 8:4, quoted at Matthew 4:4). The obedience of Jesus, in whom the human and divine natures coexist, constitutes the perfect mutual fulfillment of the law and the covenant.

"Do not say in your heart, after the LORD your God has thrust them out before you, 'It is because of my righteousness that the LORD has brought me in to possess this land'" (Deuteronomy 9:4). The Hallel Psalm rephrases this so well: "Not to us, O LORD, not to us, but to thy name give glory, for the sake of thy steadfast love and thy faithfulness!" (Psalm 115:1). Here we have the antidote to the false impression that our obedience earns us God's blessing. God blesses for the sake of His glory, because of His own goodness, and we receive the very strength for obedience as His gift.

"And the LORD was so angry with Aaron that he was ready to destroy him; and I prayed for Aaron also at the same time" (Deuteronomy 9:20). The book of Exodus leaves unclear the standing of Aaron after the debacle of the golden calf. God offered to destroy the entire people, but Moses prayed for them, and God relented. Some five thousand people were punished, but Aaron, who was the man in charge, escaped punishment. The original readers seemed to have noticed this gap in the Exodus narrative, and Deuteronomy seeks to fill it in. We learn, that the Lord was specifically angry with Aaron, but Moses saved his brother's life through intercessory prayer. Moses prayed for the wayward people in general, and for his erring brother in particular. God hears the prayer of those who pray for their siblings to be forgiven. Moses himself had to forgive his brother. And in praying for Aaron, God could not allow Moses to be more merciful than He. Forgiveness of a brother or sister is very powerful before the throne of God, and without it, none of our offerings are acceptable. "So if you are offering your gift at the altar, and there remember that your brother has something against you, leave your gift there before the altar and go; first be reconciled to your brother, and then come and offer your gift" (Matthew 5:23–24).

"Then I turned and came down from the mountain, and put the tables in the ark which I had made; and there they are, as the LORD commanded me" (Deuteronomy 10:5). Again the Deuteronomic narrative presupposes, but ever so slightly tweaks, the Exodus narrative. From this text alone, one could get the impression that Moses himself built the ark. Here, the artisans Bezalel, Oholiab, and the rest received no mention. The two books do not contradict one another, of course. Moses dictated the exact specifications of the ark, even though he left the manual labor to others who possessed the technical skills. In a similar way, one could say that the architect Frank Lloyd Wright "built" a house, while literally the descriptive verb should be "designed" a house.

Another explanation for the differences between these two passages is that Deuteronomy seeks to describe a box that Moses set aside ahead of time, as a temporary resting place for the tablets, until the divinely ordained ark could be readied. Deuteronomy may be trying to answer the quite reasonable question, "Where did Moses put the tablets, while he was waiting for the ark to be built?" As objects touched by the finger of God, they needed to be treated with the utmost reverence. In later Catholic terminology, the tablets would be considered second-class relics, objects touched by a holy person during his life, in this case touched by the Holiest One.

> First–Class Relic—bone or other remains of a saint
> *(Pieces of martyrs' bones in the altar of your church)*
>
> Second–Class Relic—object touched by a saint in life
> *(The First Holy Communion dress worn by Saint Maria Goretti)*
>
> Third–Class Relic—object touched to a saint's remains
> *(A piece of cloth touched to the tongue of Saint Anthony)*

"Circumcise therefore the foreskin of your heart, and be no longer stubborn" (Deuteronomy 10:16). Ancient Hebrews used the word *lebab* (heart) to refer to the center of human motivation, and the word *nephesh* (neck) to refer to the soul. When the heart is not in the right place, then we become stiff-necked. That is to say, our soul gets out of alignment with God. Modern people go to a chiropractor when their bones needs realignment. The Deuteronomist goes deeper, to the root of the problem, and insists that the heart needs to be circumcised. This does not refer to a surgical procedure, but to a consecration of the heart to God, so that the thoughts of the heart shall be holy. "Keep your heart with all vigilance; for from it flow the springs of life" (Proverbs 4:23). Give over your heart and your will entirely to God, who loves you and is trustworthy.

What good would be served to obey in actions, but to rebel in the heart? No human king wants mere external obedience, but rather the obeisance of a willing and devoted subject. The book of Deuteronomy is only one half-step shy of the Gospel, one split second before the Sermon on the Mount, even though they may be separated by eleven hundred years of history: "Blessed are the pure in heart, for they shall see God" (Matthew 5:8).

"For the land which you are entering to take possession of it is not like the land of Egypt, from which you have come" (Deuteronomy 11:10). The Israelites left behind the loam of Egypt, irrigated by the waters of the Nile, and set forth into the land of Canaan, which depends upon rain. Both agricultural systems depend on water, the first upon the predictable flow of the world's longest river, the other upon the less regular rainfall of the Holy Land. Farmers prefer irrigated farming to dry-land farming. Joseph's brothers went down into Egypt in the first place, to escape the drought and famine, by seeking refuge in a well-watered place. Now the Israelites leave that physical security behind for spiritual freedom. The Lord promises that He will, as part of His covenant blessing, send rain sufficient to their needs, with the understanding that they will continue to keep their part of the agreement. Some of the psalms appeal to this divine promise and constitute prayers for rain: "The voice of the LORD is upon the waters; the God of glory thunders, the LORD, upon many waters" (Psalm 29:3).

Some students of the law interpreted such passages to mean that whenever it rains, God is pleased and whenever there is drought, He is displeased. That would reduce God to a mere rain god, like Tlaloc among the Aztecs or Thor among the Saxons. Jesus gives the corrective to this misunderstanding: "Be sons of your Father who is in heaven; for he makes his sun rise on the evil and on the good, and sends rain on the just and on the unjust" (Matthew 5:45). God gives the blessing of life to all people, both those who use it wisely and those who do not. Therefore, He blesses all and curses no one. His special blessing, however, is upon those whom He charges with special tasks. "Every one to whom much is given, of him will much be required" (Luke 12:48). God's special care was with the Hebrews, for they would bring forth the Redeemer.

"Set the blessing on Mount Gerizim and the curse on Mount Ebal" (Deuteronomy 11:29). Mount Gerizim is an important pinnacle in the very middle of the Holy Land, midway between Jerusalem and Galilee. The Samaritans maintained that mount as the holy place intended by Almighty God, and not Jerusalem, which is never mentioned in the promises to Moses. After the death of Moses, Joshua leads the people of Israel across the Jordan River and puts half the people on Mount Gerizim to utter the blessings of the Torah, and the other half of the people on nearby Mount Ebal to pronounce the curses (Joshua 8:33). Samaritans maintained that as a result, Gerizim is blessed, while Ebal is cursed. To counter this claim, Jewish apologists answered that the blessings uttered on Gerizim were directed towards Ebal, while the curses voiced on Ebal were directed towards Gerizim, and therefore Mount Gerizim became the cursed mountain.

Jesus settles the matter definitively, when He meets the Samaritan woman and, under the shadow of Mount Gerizim, declares "Woman, believe me, the hour is coming when neither on this mountain nor in Jerusalem will you worship the Father. You worship what you do not know; we worship what we know, for salvation is from the Jews. But the hour is coming, and now is, when the true worshipers will worship the Father in spirit and truth, for such the Father seeks to worship him. God is spirit, and those who worship him must worship in spirit and truth" (John 4:21–24).

The true believer worships God faithfully in love and obedience. Blessings from God precede and follow obedience, in good times and in difficult times, until the pilgrimage in this world is over and a world of blessing awaits him in heaven.

As Saint John says: *The law was given through Moses, grace and truth came through Jesus Christ.* In Him the promise made through the shadows of prophecy stands revealed, along with the full meaning of the precepts of the law. He is the one who teaches the truth of prophecy through His presence, and makes obedience to the commandments possible through grace.

(Pope Saint Leo the Great [reigned AD 440–61], *Sermon 51, 3–4, 8*)

1. How should the Israelites deal with the pagans? Deuteronomy 7:1–5

2. Why did God bring the Israelites out of slavery? Deuteronomy 7:6–8

3. What can you learn about the nature and character of God?

Deuteronomy 7:8–10	
Psalm 119:160	
CCC 215	

4. Why did God reveal Himself to Israel?

Deuteronomy 7:8	
CCC 218	

5. List some of the blessings of obedience to God. Deuteronomy 7:11–26

6. How long did the Israelites' clothing and shoes last? Deuteronomy 8:4

7. Identify some types and sources of hunger from the following passages.

Deuteronomy 8:3–5	
Amos 8:11–12	
Luke 4:1–4	
John 6:35, 48–51	
CCC 2835	

8. Can you identify a time in your life when you were spiritually hungry? How was that hunger satisfied?

9. Explain some dangers of blessing and prosperity. Deuteronomy 8:6–20

* Can you think of a contemporary example of this danger?

10. Why did God give Israel success and blessings? Deuteronomy 9:5–6

11. In your own words explain the drama in the following passages.

Deuteronomy 9:7–14	
Deuteronomy 9:15–17	
Deuteronomy 9:18–20	
Deuteronomy 9:21	
Deuteronomy 9:22–24	
Deuteronomy 9:25–29	
Deuteronomy 10:1–5	

12. What does God require of us?

Deuteronomy 10:12	
Deuteronomy 10:13	
Deuteronomy 10:19	
Deuteronomy 10:20	
Micah 6:8	

13. Paraphrase Deuteronomy 10:16 into modern English that you could act upon.

14. Explain five ways you could sin against God's love. CCC 2094

Indifference	

15. Which of the above could be a source of temptation for you?

16. What does God command in Deuteronomy 11:1?

17. Describe the blessing for obedience found in Deuteronomy 11:8–9.

18. Compare the following promises and blessings.

Deuteronomy 11:13–16	
Psalm 104:14–15	

19. What can you learn from the following passages?

Deuteronomy 11:18–23	
CCC 2223	
CCC 2225	
CCC 2226	

20. Share a situation or specific time in your life when you were obedient to God, and experienced His blessing.

Chapter 19

Kosher Law
Deuteronomy 12–20

**You are a people holy to the Lord your God,
and the Lord has chosen you to be a people for his own possession,
out of all the peoples that are on the face of the earth.**
Deuteronomy 14:2

In the beginning of the Torah in the Garden of Eden, God gave Adam and Eve permission to eat as vegetarians. "Behold, I have given you every plant yielding seed which is upon the face of the earth, and every tree with seed in its fruit; you shall have them for food" (Genesis 1:29). The only restriction that God imposed was against the fruit of one single tree. "You may freely eat of every tree of the garden; but of the tree of the knowledge of good and evil you shall not eat, for in the day that you eat of it you shall die" (Genesis 2:16). Only after the Flood, did God explicitly expand the human diet to include meat. "Every moving thing that lives shall be food for you; and as I gave you the green plants, I give you everything. Only you shall not eat flesh with its life, that is, its blood" (Genesis 9:3–4).

Since the time of Noah many social taboos have arisen in connection with the preparation and consumption of food. According to the food sources available in various quarters of the planet, the local people have learned to make do with different sources of nutrition. Northern Europeans drink beer; southern Europeans drink wine. Southern Indians consume rice; northern Indians eat wheat bread. Southern Chinese like sweet sauces; northern Chinese prefer hot sauces.

Europeans sometimes eat horsemeat, without any qualms at all. In America, however, where the horse acted as partner on the old frontier, the eating of any horse, young, middle-aged, or old, is considered inherently repulsive. Old horses went to the glue factory, but not to the slaughterhouse. The United States Congress enacted legislation to forbid the sale of horsemeat for consumption, and later added a provision banning the export of horses for consumption elsewhere.

Every people on the face of the earth have specific ideas of how to define food. The Mosaic code is unique in legislating a complete set of instructions for preparation, cooking, and serving of food, as well as cleanup afterwards. No other ancient code bothers to discuss the question of food in any detail; they leave the question of diet to social custom without finding expression in the law.

The Hebrew term, *kosher,* which means "proper" or "right," describes the food permitted by the Torah, along with the appropriate cooking and serving utensils. The opposite of *kosher* is "torn," taken from the following passage, which prohibits the consumption of fat. "You shall eat no fat, of ox, or sheep, or goat. The fat of an animal that dies of itself, and the fat of one that is torn by beasts, may be put to any other use, but on not account shall you eat it" (Leviticus 7:22).

"You shall not eat the blood" (Deuteronomy 12:16). The general dispensation to Noah already mentioned not eating meat with the blood still in it. The punishment for eating blood is excommunication from the people. "Moreover you shall eat no blood whatever, whether of fowl or of animal, in any of your dwellings. Whoever eats any blood, that person shall be cut off from his people" (Leviticus 7:26–27).

Kosher law comes into force with the act of slaughter. The favored method is slitting the animal's throat, which is considered a mercifully quick death, and an efficient method of draining the blood. Moslems as well as Jews hang the sides of meat to drain slowly. Kosher meats are also submitted to boiling and other cooking methods that remove what blood remains.

With the removal of fat and blood, meats certified as kosher are lean and healthy cuts that any dietician could approve for cardiovascular patients. The Torah does not give a health reason for this, or any other of the kosher statutes, however. In fact, there is only one kosher law for which a clear reason has been given: "For the life of the flesh is in the blood; and I have given it for you upon the altar to make atonement for your souls; for it is the blood that makes atonement by reason of the life" (Leviticus 17:11). Deuteronomy provides another reason: "Only be sure that you do not eat the blood; for the blood is the life, and you shall not eat the life with the flesh. You shall not eat it; you shall pour it out upon the earth like water. You shall not eat it; that all may go well with you and with your children after you, when you do what is right in the sight of the LORD (Deuteronomy 12:23–25).

"You shall not eat any abominable thing" (Deuteronomy 14:3). Deuteronomy gives the fullest enumeration of the clean and unclean animals, birds, and fish. Of these, fish have the simplest set of rules. "Of all that are in the waters you may eat these: Whatever has fins and scales you may eat. And whatever does not have fins and scales you shall not eat" (Deuteronomy 14:9–10). The fishermen on the Sea of Galilee put out their nets at night and hauled in different kinds of species, some of which were kosher, and some "torn." In the morning, they would spread out their catch on the shore and separate the clean from the unclean—clean for sale to the Jews and unclean for sale to the Gentiles. So, the apostles Peter, Andrew, James, and John were keenly aware of the kosher rules. Their business required supplying each separate community with what was required for their respective diets.

Bird species, which fell on carcasses, are considered unclean. Their contact with all kinds of dead bodies, including unclean animals, makes them unsuitable for human consumption. Who would regret the inclusion of bats among forbidden flying creatures, though they are mammals rather than birds? Nor will the exclusion of winged insects make anyone feel deprived. Any bird not specifically forbidden is permitted. "You may eat all clean birds" (Deuteronomy 14:11). However, some Jews today do not eat turkey, because they consider it questionable—related to the chicken, which is clean, or to the ostrich, which is unclean?

The most complicated category is the animal that walks on land. Clean animals both chew the cud and are cloven hoofed—ox, sheep, goat, hart, gazelle, roebuck, wild goat, ibex, antelope, and mountain sheep. Considered unclean are cud-chewing animals without cloven hoofs—camel, hare, and rock-badger.

Considered especially unclean is the swine, which is cloven hoofed, but does not chew the cud. "Their flesh you shall not eat, and their carcasses you shall not touch" (Deuteronomy 14:8). Muslims and Jews both refuse to touch pigs, eat their flesh, or even use their lard. When the prodigal son was reduced to tending pigs, his fall from grace was complete (Luke 15:15). When Jesus entered the Gerasene territory, inhabited by Gentiles, He saw a heard of swine, and sent a legion of demons into them, where-upon they drowned themselves in the sea (Matthew 8:32).

"You shall not boil a kid in its mother's milk" (Deuteronomy 14:21). One of the fundamental rules of kosher diet is never to combine a dairy product with meat in the same meal. Some reports indicate that the consumption of milk and meat together inhibits digestion, but the reason for this statute may be compassion for the animal that gave the milk and not to consume both the gift and the giver at once. Even that does not explain the scrupulosity of the kosher kitchen, which has two sets of utensils, one for dairy and one for meat, and they cannot be washed together.

Some rabbis say that the purpose of the kosher laws was to make it difficult for Jews and Gentiles to eat together. Whether or not that was the intention, it certainly is the effect. Gentiles can always eat Jewish food, of course, but not vice versa. For this reason, Saint Peter exempted the Christians from the kosher laws of the Mosaic code, so that Jewish Christians and Gentile Christians could share the Eucharist along with agape and ordinary meals (Acts 10:15).

"At the end of every seven years you shall grant a release" (Deuteronomy 15:1). The Jewish calendar divides itself into weeks of years as well as weeks of days. Just as every seventh day is a sabbath to the Lord, so every seventh year is a jubilee. Creditors must forgive all debts at the end of that year, so that indebtedness can never accumulate for longer than 84 months. Jesus certainly has this requirement in mind, when He instructs His followers to pray: "And forgive us our debts, as we also have forgiven our debtors" (Matthew 6:12). Elsewhere, He explains, "If you lend to those from whom you hope to receive, what credit is that to you? Even sinners lend to sinners, to receive as much again. But love your enemies, and do good, and lend, expecting nothing in return; and your reward will be great, and you will be sons of the Most High" (Luke 6:34–35).

To lend is merciful, but to hold the debtor in the yoke of long-term debt is a form of servitude. For that reason, the Mosaic code allows only short-term loans. In the first year of the week of years, a six-year loan is possible, but in the last year of the week of years, only a one-year loan is possible.

During ancient times, people often became slaves because of debts they could not repay. Therefore, the Mosaic code orders that Hebrew slaves may never serve longer than seven years (Deuteronomy 15:12), counted from whenever the servitude began, so that all slaves are not emancipated simultaneously. Again the code stays shy of abolishing slavery altogether, but imposes humanizing limits upon it. On the seventh day of the week, no master may give an order to any slave, and that adds up to 313 days of servitude a year. In the seventh year of servitude, each slave must be set free, and so no slave in ancient Israel had to submit to more than 2191 days of servile labor in a seven-year period of service.

"You shall count seven weeks" (Deuteronomy 16:9). The period of time from Passover to Pentecost comprises seven weeks, or fifty days. The Greek word "Pentecost" refers to the fifty-day period between the two feasts. The period between the feasts is a week of weeks, and so the Hebrew name for Pentecost is the Feast of Weeks. The Book of Leviticus similarly established a jubilee every fiftieth year, which is the period seven year-weeks. Every seventh year of release is to be a time of general release. "And you shall hallow the fiftieth year, and proclaim liberty throughout the land to all its inhabitants" (Leviticus 25:10).

When Pope Boniface VIII instituted the first Papal Jubilee in the year AD 1300, he intended the holy year to take place every fifty years. Vatican officials discovered that period to be so long that hardly anyone could remember what happened the last time, and soon the Papal Jubilees came to be every 25 years. The biggest jubilee in history was the Millenium Jubilee of 2000, when 25 million pilgrims came to visit the shrines in Rome. At that time, Pope John Paul II stood in the great tradition of the Hebrew jubilee when he appealed to wealthy countries to forgive the debts of third-world nations.

"Your eye shall not pity; it shall be life for life" (Deuteronomy 19:21). Abruptly, after the merciful prior legislation, the harsh prescription of the talonic law reasserts itself for the third time in the Torah. "Your eye shall not pity; it shall be life for life, eye for eye, tooth for tooth, hand for hand, foot for foot" (Deuteronomy 19:21).

A longer form of the talonic litany was found in the first instance in the Book of Exodus. "If any harm follows, then you shall give life for life, eye for eye, tooth for tooth, hand for hand, foot for foot, burn for burn, wound for wound, stripe for stripe" (Exodus 21:23–24).

A second short form appeared in the Book of Leviticus. "When a man causes disfigurement in his neighbor, as he has done it shall be done to him, fracture for fracture, eye for eye, tooth for tooth, as he has disfigured a man, he shall be disfigured (Leviticus 24:19–20).

Commentators explain that other systems of law required the death penalty for nearly everything, while the Mosaic law forbids exacting more than proportional satisfaction. In fact, the Code of Hammurabi (nos. 196, 197, and 200) contains a section of laws very similar to those in the Torah: "If a seignior has destroyed the eye of a member of the aristocracy, they shall destroy his eye. If he has broken another seignior's bone, they shall break his bone. ... If a seignior has knocked out the tooth of a seignior of his own rank, they shall knock out his tooth." (James B. Pritchard, *Ancient Near Eastern Texts Relating to the Old Testament* [Princeton, NJ: University Press, 1950], p. 175).

This formula looks like justice, but it actually perpetuates a cycle of violence that has repeated itself down through history from the time of Cain and Abel. The human race needs to be liberated, not just from external violence, but also from the internal imperative of revenge. Only Jesus Christ provides the definitive alternative to this kind of law in His Sermon on the Mount: "You have heard that it was said, 'An eye for an eye and a tooth for a tooth.' But I say to you, Do not resist one who is evil. But if any one strikes you on the right cheek, turn to him the other also" (Matthew 5:38–39).

1. Where does God expect to be worshipped? Deuteronomy 12:1–14

2. What does God offer, and with what stipulation in Deuteronomy 12:15–28?

3. Why is it wrong to partake of blood? Deuteronomy 12:23–25

4. Describe some penalties for idolatry. Deuteronomy 13

5. Make a list of clean and unclean animals, fish, and birds. Deuteronomy 14:3-20

	Clean	Unclean
Animals		
Fish		
Birds		

6. What practice is commanded in Deuteronomy 14:22–28.

7. What can you learn from the following passages?

Deuteronomy 15:1–11	
John 12:8	
CCC 2449	

8. What do you do, on a regular basis, for the poor?

9. How should slaves be treated? Deuteronomy 15:12–18

10. Why should Jews treat slaves considerately? Deuteronomy 15:15

11. Which feasts are discussed in the following passages?

Deuteronomy 16:1–8	
Deuteronomy 16:9–12	
Deuteronomy 16:13–17	

12. Why is true justice important? Deuteronomy 16:18–20

13. What is the New Testament significance of the Deuteronomy passage below?

Deuteronomy 17:6–7	
Matthew 18:15–17	
John 8:17–20	

14. Was Mosaic Law (Deuteronomy 17:6–7) obeyed in the trials of Jesus Christ?

Matthew 26:59–63	
Mark 14:55–56	
John 18:29–40	

15. List some admonitions for a king. Deuteronomy 17:14–20

16. What practices are condemned in Deuteronomy 18:9–12?

** List some contemporary forms or manifestations of divination.

17. What does the Catholic Church teach about forms of divination? CCC 2116

18. Describe the crime committed in Deuteronomy 19:11–13.

19. Compare the following verses.

Deuteronomy 19:14	
Proverbs 23:10	
Hosea 5:10	

20. What considerations offer exemptions from serving in war? Deuteronomy 20

** How often do you need sanctification? CCC 2813

Mosaic Marriage Laws
Deuteronomy 21–26

**You shall be careful to perform what has passed your lips,
for you have voluntarily vowed to the LORD your God
what you have promised with your mouth.**
Deuteronomy 23:23

The Importance of Marriage in God's Plan — From the very first chapters of the Bible, God reveals the importance of marriage, the one flesh union between one man and one woman for life, in His plan. Even in the Garden of Eden, evil attacks the perfect plan. Sin introduces a host of problems onto the stage of human affairs. Murder, adultery, lying, stealing, rape, covetousness, and divorce demand a response. Most sexual sins lead to shattered lives for innocent victims. In the Torah a variety of laws are established to deal with these evils. In fact, the Mosaic law contains many regulations that seek to protect both the sanctity of marriage and the victims of sinful sexual practices.

Marriage and the family are rooted in the inmost nucleus of the truth about man and his destiny. Sacred Scripture reveals that the vocation to love is part of the authentic image of God, which the Creator has desired to impress upon his creature[s], calling them to resemble him precisely to the extent in which they are open to love. …

Corresponding to the image of a monotheistic God is a monogamous marriage. Marriage based on exclusive and definitive love becomes the icon of the relationship between God and his people and vice versa. …Today, the need to avoid confusing **marriage** with other types of unions based on weak love is especially urgent. It is only the rock of total, irrevocable love between a man and a woman that can serve as the foundation on which to build a society that will become a home for all mankind.

Pope Benedict XVI,
Address to the Pontifical John Paul II Institute, May 11, 2006.

Anthropologists have a general rule that the more widespread a practice is among cultures, the more ancient it must be. The fact that marriage is a social institution found everywhere, in all cultures and all places, means that it is very ancient. It must go back to the beginning of the human race. Genesis, the first book of the Torah, concurs with this hypothesis in the creation account. "God created man in his own image, in the image of God he created him; male and female he created them. And God blessed them, and God said to them, 'Be fruitful and multiply'" (Genesis 1:27–28). Later, the same book adds, "Therefore a man leaves his father and his mother and cleaves to his wife, and they become one flesh" (Genesis 2:24).

Jesus gives a definitive interpretation of these passages. "So they are no longer two but one. What therefore God has joined together, let man not put asunder" (Matthew 19:6). In these few words, Jesus establishes conclusively that marriage is both monogamous (one wife per man), and indissoluble (until death parts them).

Some Mosaic laws regarding marriage dealt with specific problems in antiquity. For example, marrying a female captive and introducing her into the community posed special challenges. Other laws dealt with covetousness and the need to keep a family's land and property in the family. So, if a widow had no children, her brother-in-law would marry her to provide sons for her, and to keep the land in the family.

Sexual sins damage marriage and threaten family life. Human cultures have developed different customs surrounding courtship, weddings, and married life. Some practices are true to the nature of marriage but others are false. Some Hebrew patriarchs practiced polygamy, for example. However, the Torah does not condone polygamy. Indeed, the strife between Jacob's twelve sons stems precisely from the fact that they have four different mothers. By the time of Moses, polygamy seems to have waned, perhaps because the Egyptians, among whom they sojourned, held a high monogamous standard.

"If a man has two wives, the one loved and the other disliked" (Deuteronomy 21:15) — The Deuteronomist assumes that polygamy causes trouble in the home, not only between the man and his wives, but also between the man and his sons. "If the first-born son is hers that is disliked ... he may not treat the son of the loved as the first-born in preference to the son of the disliked (Deuteronomy 21:15–16). Apart from this passage, polygamy is rarely mentioned in the matrimonial legislation of the Torah. The Deuteronomist treats polygamy as rare and troublesome.

Polygamy is still legal under Islamic law throughout the Middle East. A Muslim man may take up to four wives, providing he can afford them. While Christian and Jewish men in those lands, no matter how wealthy, are expected to remain faithful to a single wife. Monogamy offers dignity to the woman, financial integrity for the family, harmony between offspring, and peace of mind for the husband and wife. Common sense favors monogamy, even where polygamy is permitted by civil law.

Adultery and Fornication — Deuteronomy 22:22 prescribes the penalty of death by stoning for both the man and woman involved in the sin of *adultery*—sexual relations between married people who are married to others. Deuteronomy 22:24 assigns the same death penalty for the sin of *fornication*—sexual relations between unmarried people. However, in Deuteronomy 22:26, a maiden who is raped outside of the city is vindicated and freed, because she could not call out for help. Only the rapist will die. In Muslim law, only the adulterous *woman* is subject to the death penalty, but in Mosaic and other ancient systems of law, both the adulterer and the adulteress must die. The Code of Hammurabi directed that an adulterer and adulteress be bound together and thrown into the sea.

Mosaic law specifies that a man who has sexual relations with a virgin must pay his future father-in-law fifty silver shekels to marry her, and he may not divorce her as long as he lives. Since the customary bride price at that time was only thirty shekels, the man is being punished for not behaving honorably toward the virgin and marrying her before having intercourse with her.

Ancient codes of law dealt extensively with adultery. The certainty of bloodlines was of paramount importance to their societies. No test for paternity existed except the unimpeachable integrity of the mother. Any act of adultery called into question the inheritance rights of her children, and so women were strongly motivated to avoid even the appearance of impropriety.

The sixth commandment says simply, "You shall not commit adultery" (Exodus 20:14). The subsequent legislation of Deuteronomy reveals that this commandment exists to protect the purity of the unmarried as well as married persons. The bride who is found to no longer be a virgin on her wedding night, is subject to the death penalty at the door of her father's house, "because she has wrought folly in Israel by playing the harlot in her father's house" (Deuteronomy 22:21). The logic here is that the married woman who commits adultery is false to her husband, while the unmarried woman is doubly false—both to her father and to her future husband.

Penalties differ from one culture to another. The Code of Hammurabi, Number 128 provides: "If the wife of a seignior has been caught while lying with another man, they shall bind them and throw them into the water. If the husband of the woman wishes to spare his wife, then the king in turn may spare his subject" (James B. Pritchard, *Ancient Near Eastern Texts Relating to the Old Testament* [Princeton, NJ: University Press, 1950], p. 171). The Middle Assyrian Laws make no such provision for clemency; both are put to death.

Even in the stricter juridical systems, public punishment only resulted when private mercy was withheld. Joseph could have had the Blessed Virgin Mary stoned to death for being with child, but instead, he resolved to divorce her quietly, a resort to mercy rather than to justice (Matthew 1:19). The Christian tradition emphasizes forgiveness and mercy towards sinners. So, Jesus tells the men who plan to stone an adulteress, "Let him who is without sin among you be the first to cast a stone at her." He tells the adulteress, "Go, and do not sin again" (John 8:7, 11). To forgive is not to condone sin, but to hate the sin is truly to love the sinner as Jesus did.

Divorce — Writing a bill of divorce was an ancient practice among certain cultures. The Code of Hammurabi required that a man return the full marriage price and the dowry brought from her father's house to his wife, before a divorce. Greek and Roman women had few civil rights. The Torah speaks obliquely about divorce. Levites may not marry divorced women (Leviticus 21:14). A Levite's divorced daughter may return to her father's home (Leviticus 22:13). Divorced women may make vows (Numbers 30:9). A man who divorces his wife is prohibited from re-marrying her after she has been married to someone else (Deuteronomy 24:3). The man might find his ex-wife to be more attractive considering the property she may have amassed with her second husband. Other than these few points, the Torah is silent. The history of Israel has not chronicled a single instance of divorce among kings or commoners. One may surmise that divorce is tolerated, but not approved.

While divorce was practiced in antiquity, this practice was never part of God's perfect plan. God observed divorce, but He did not plan it. God instituted marriage as a stable, life-long institution. The Prophet Malachi expresses God's intention. "So take heed to yourselves, and let none be faithless to the wife of his youth. 'For I hate divorce,' says the LORD the God of Israel" (Malachi 2:15–16).

Jesus confirms this sentiment. "They said, 'Moses allowed a man to write a certificate of divorce, and to put her away. But Jesus said to them, 'For your hardness of heart he wrote you this commandment. … What therefore God has joined together, let not man put asunder'" (Mark 10:4–9). Catholic teaching and practice attempt to implement the clear teaching of Jesus, while offering assistance to couples at every stage of their relationship. By the grace of God, matrimony is a holy sacrament.

Guard the sanctity of marriage; pray and work for strong, solid, healthy, loving, life-affirming marriages. At the same time, show compassion for those who have been the victims of the sins and betrayals of others. God hates the sin and loves the sinner. Christians are compelled to follow the example of Christ. Speak the truth in love. Encourage spouses to remain faithful to one another in good times and bad. Help married persons to seek God's help in weathering the storms of family life. The Catholic Church offers *Marriage Encounters* to support strong marriages, and *Retrouvaille* to minister to those in troubled marriages.

God knows the sorrow of betrayed and abandoned spouses, whose marriage vows have been broken. God sees the pain of children, siblings, grandparents, relatives, and friends, who watch helplessly as a marriage and family are torn apart. The Church also grieves at the assaults on marriage and family life that wound individuals, families, and society as a whole.

Children — The importance of marriage and family life in God's plan can be seen clearly in the laws dealing with an incorrigible child (Deuteronomy 21:18–21). What kind of parent would send a rebellious child to the elders of the city? And yet that is exactly what parents in contemporary society, who refuse to train and discipline their children, do. For when the parents refuse to train and discipline their child, then the teachers must try to do it. And if the teachers fail, then the employers must do it. And if the employers fail, then the police and the courts must do it. The destruction of the family contributes to overcrowded prisons and jails. A healthy society requires healthy families.

The Culture — The admonition to "purge evil from your midst" remains relevant. There are so many areas in contemporary society, in which the culture has failed to purge the evil, which remains to destroy. Drug addiction, pornography, and gang activities are a few examples of the evils that thrive, at the society's peril. Drug lords get rich, while children die of overdoses. Turning one's back on evil does not make it go away. The evil simply festers until it erupts at another time.

Perhaps the whole idea of these various laws strikes an uneasy chord in our culture. Yet, if God is not the arbitrator of right and wrong, then society is left to its own whims. One obvious characteristic of western society is narcissism. Cultural relativism has become a norm. "If it feels good, it must be good. If it seems right for you, it must be right. Moreover, somehow what is true for one person may not be true for another?" This confusion encourages the contemporary person to place himself as the sole judge and arbitrator of truth and goodness, rather than Almighty God.

In such an environment, it becomes increasingly difficult to accept God's Word in submission and docility. Because God is God, He sees the whole picture. God was there from the beginning. He will exist for all eternity. Man has questions. God has answers. If passages in Sacred Scripture seem difficult or harsh, man is tempted to judge God. This is a very dangerous and futile position.

Ezekiel learned this lesson.

> "Yet you say, 'The way of the LORD is not just.' Hear now, O house of Israel: Is my way not just? Is it not your ways that are not just? When a righteous man turns away from his righteousness and commits iniquity, he shall die for it; for the iniquity which he has committed he shall die. Again, when a wicked man turns away from the wickedness he has committed and does what is lawful and right, he shall save his life. Because he considered and turned away from all the transgressions which he had committed, he shall surely live, he shall not die. Yet the house of Israel says, 'The way of the LORD is not just. O house of Israel, are my ways not just? Is it not your ways that are not just?
>
> Therefore I will judge you, O house of Israel, every one according to his ways, says the LORD GOD. Repent and turn from all your transgressions, lest iniquity be your ruin. Cast away from you all the transgressions which you have committed against me, and get yourselves a new heart and a new spirit! Why will you die, O house of Israel? For I have no pleasure in the death of any one, says the LORD GOD; so turn, and live."
>
> Ezekiel 18:25–32

If a law or precept of the Lord seems harsh or confusing, pray for humility and docility. God is a good God. His ways are just and merciful. Trust in God alone. The many marriage laws attempt to protect the same institution that is the bedrock of society today, and which still warrants protection.

"Her husband's brother shall go in to her" (Deuteronomy 25:5). The institution of the levirate marriage existed to perpetuate the family, so that when a man died before he was able to beget an heir, the next of kin would fulfill this responsibility. Biblical instances of this kind of marriage may be found in the case of Judah's daughter-in-law Tamar in Genesis 38, and of Naomi's daughter-in-law Ruth in the Book of Ruth.

The Sadducees refer to this practice when they question Jesus, asking whose wife such a woman would be, who had married as many as seven brothers. This provides Jesus with the opportunity to give another teaching on marriage. He says, "For in the resurrection they neither marry nor are given in marriage, but are like angels in heaven" (Matthew 22:30). Marriage is an earthly institution, established so that men and women may help each other on their paths to heaven, and populate the earth with future citizens of heaven. But, once heaven is attained, the needs of earth no longer pertain. Heaven will be the wedding feast of the Lamb, Jesus Christ, married to His Church for all eternity. "And the angel said to me, 'Write this: Blessed are those who are invited to the marriage supper of the Lamb'" (Revelation 19:9).

The family is an intermediate institution between individuals and society, and nothing can completely take its place. The family is itself based primarily on a deep interpersonal relationship between husband and wife, sustained by affection and mutual understanding. To enable this, it receives abundant help from God in the sacrament of Matrimony, which brings with it a true vocation to holiness …

The family is a necessary good for peoples, an indispensable foundation for society and a great and lifelong treasure for couples. It is a unique good for children, who are meant to be the fruit of the love, of the total and generous self-giving of their parents. To proclaim the whole truth about the family, based on marriage as *a domestic Church and a sanctuary of life,* is a great responsibility incumbent upon all.

Father and mother have said a complete "yes" in the sight of God, which constitutes the basis of the sacrament which joins them together. Likewise, for the inner relationship of the family to be complete, they also need to say a "yes" of acceptance to the children whom they have given birth to or adopted, and each of which has his or her own personality and character. In this way, children will grow up in a climate of acceptance and love, and upon reaching sufficient maturity, will then want to say "yes" in turn to those who gave them life.

Pope Benedict XVI,
Address to the World Meeting of Families, July 8, 2006.

1. On finding a dead body in the open land, what should God's chosen ones do? Deuteronomy 21:1–9

2. Explain the laws for a man wanting to marry a captive. Deuteronomy 21:10–14

3. What are the rights of the first-born son of a man who no longer loves his wife? Deuteronomy 21:15–17

4. Why would an incorrigible child be treated so severely as to be stoned in Israel? Deuteronomy 21:21

5. How was the curse of the law broken, and by whom?

Deuteronomy 21:22–23	
Galatians 3:13–14	

6. List some ways to treat others' property or animals. Deuteronomy 22:1–4

7. Complete the chart of various precepts below.

Deuteronomy 22:5	
Deuteronomy 22:6–7	
Deuteronomy 22:8	
Deuteronomy 22:9–11	
Deuteronomy 22:12	

8. If you obey these precepts of the Lord, what can result? Deuteronomy 22:7b

9. Explain the following crimes against marriage and the various punishments.

Deuteronomy 22:13–19	
Deuteronomy 22:20–21	
Deuteronomy 22:22	
Deuteronomy 22:23–24	
Deuteronomy 22:25–27	
Deuteronomy 22:28–29	
Deuteronomy 22:30 RSVCE Deuteronomy 23:1 NAB	

10. What does the Christian sacrament of Matrimony entail? CCC 1601

11. Explain the presence of polygamy and divorce in the Bible. CCC 1610

12. Why would some people be excluded from the assembly of the Lord? Deuteronomy 23:1–9

13. Why are cleanliness and hygiene important to Israel? Deuteronomy 23:10–15

14. Describe the following precepts of the Lord.

Deuteronomy 23:16–17	
Deuteronomy 23:18–19	
Deuteronomy 23:20–21	
Luke 6:34–36	
Deuteronomy 23:22–24	
Deuteronomy 23:25–26	

15. Explain the following laws. Discuss possible reasons for these laws.

Deuteronomy 24:1–4	
Deuteronomy 24:5	
Deuteronomy 24:6	
Deuteronomy 24:7	
Deuteronomy 24:8–9	
Deuteronomy 24:10–13	
Deuteronomy 24:14–15	
CCC 2434	
Deuteronomy 24:16	
Deuteronomy 24:17–18	
Deuteronomy 24:19–22	

16. What happens when you show charity to the poor? Deuteronomy 24:13b

17. Explain the following passages.

Deuteronomy 25:1–3	
2 Corinthians 11:24	
Deuteronomy 25:4	
1 Timothy 5:17–18	

18. Clarify the importance of honesty. Deuteronomy 25:13–16

19. How should one respond to God's goodness?

Deuteronomy 26:1–11	
Deuteronomy 26:12–16	

20. Explain God's Covenant with His people. Deuteronomy 26:16–19

* With your small group, brainstorm ways to strengthen marriages today. Pray, affirm, encourage, work at it, etc. Then do some of them.

CHAPTER 21

Blessings and Curses
Deuteronomy 27–30

**Blessed shall you be when you come in,
and blessed shall you be when you go out.**
Deuteronomy 28:6

God's covenant with Abraham involved both blessing and curse. "I will bless you, and make your name great, so that you will be a blessing. I will bless those who bless you, and him who curses you I will curse; and by you all the families of the earth shall bless themselves" (Genesis 12:2–3).

One should not be surprised then, that the Mosaic covenant also involves both the blessing and the curse. "Behold, I set before you this day a blessing and a curse: the blessing, if you obey the commandments of the LORD your God, which I command you this day, and the curse, if you do not obey the commandments of the LORD your God, but turn aside from the way which I command you this day, to go after other gods which you have not known" (Deuteronomy 11:26–28).

The Egyptians inscribed curses on the entryways of their tombs, to deter grave robbers. During the Sixth Dynasty, the official Meni wrote the following curse on the entry of his tomb at Giza: "The crocodile be against him in the water, the snake be against him on land—(against) him who may do a thing to this (tomb). I never did a thing to him. It is the god who will judge (him)" (James B. Pritchard, *Ancient Near Eastern Texts Relating to the Old Testament* [Princeton, NJ: University Press, 1950], p. 327).

Other peoples in the Middle East did the same to protect their tombs. The sarcophagus of King Hiram of Byblos bears one of the earliest inscriptions in the Phoenician alphabet. "The coffin which Ittobaal, son of Ahiram, king of Byblos, made for his father as his abode in eternity. And if any king or any governor or any army commander attack Byblos and expose this coffin, let his judicial scepter be broken, let his royal throne be overthrown, and let peace flee from Byblos; and as for him, let a vagabond efface his inscriptions!" (Stanislav Segert, *A Grammar of Pheonician and Punic* [Munich, Germany: C.H. Beck, 1975], p. 267).

The Torah uses two different Hebrew nouns to designate a curse:
* *Alah* is an "oath, execration, imprecation," and appears three times in Numbers (Numbers 5:21, 23, and 27) and four times in Deuteronomy (Deuteronomy 29:19, 20, 21, and 30:7).
* *Qelalah* is "a reviling, a thing lightly esteemed," and appears twice in Genesis (Genesis 27:12 and 13) and nine times in Deuteronomy (Deuteronomy 11:26, 28, and 29; 23:5; 27:13; 28:15 and 45; 29:27; and 30:1). This word often occurs in contrast

with the word *barakah,* "blessing." Moses gives instructions to the people that, after their entrance into the Promised Land, half the tribes will stand on Mount Gerizim to bless the people, and the other half will stand on the facing Mount Ebal for the curses. Moses specifies in Deuteronomy 27:12–13 which tribe will stand on each mountain:

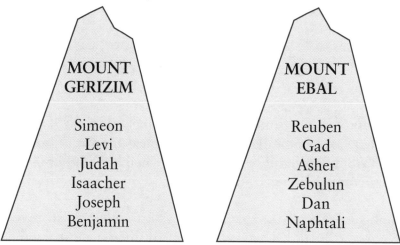

MOUNT GERIZIM

Simeon
Levi
Judah
Isaacher
Joseph
Benjamin

MOUNT EBAL

Reuben
Gad
Asher
Zebulun
Dan
Naphtali

In general, the tribes who descend from Jacob's wives appear on Mount Gerizim, while those who descend from the sons of concubines are stationed on Mount Ebal. Both sons of Rachel, the favored wife, are on the mount of blessing (Joseph and Benjamin). The six sons of Leah are divided up, four on the mount of blessing (Simeon, Levi, Judah, and Issachar), and the other two on Mount Ebal (Reuben and Zebulun). The sons of the two concubines are grouped together on the mountain of cursing (Gad, Asher, Dan, and Naphtali). The presence of Levi on Mount Gerizim is especially appropriate because one of the principle functions of the priestly tribe is to bless the people in the name of the Lord. The Aaronic blessing reads: "The LORD bless and keep you; the LORD make his face to shine upon you, and be gracious to you: The LORD lift up his countenance upon you, and give you peace" (Numbers 6:24–26).

Oddly, then, the Book of Deuteronomy (Deuteronomy 27:14) puts into the mouths of the Levites a recitation of the twelve curses—oddly because priests are supposed to bless in general, and oddly also because the tribe of Levi was assigned to stand on the Gerizim of blessings rather than on the Ebal of curses. Scholars agree that part of the text here is missing, lost during the long period of transmission. The curses have survived, but the blessings have gotten lost along the way!

"Cursed be he who removes his neighbor's landmark" (Deuteronomy 27:17). The twelve curses in the Book of Deuteronomy (Deuteronomy 27:15–23) recapitulate the values already contained in the Decalogue, and apply those general norms in a few more specific ways. For example, the third curse promulgates a new statute that did not appear yet in the Torah, "In the inheritance which you will hold in the land that the LORD your God gives you to possess, you shall not remove your neighbor's landmark, which the men of old have set" (Deuteronomy 19:14). This statute applies the commandment, "Neither shall you steal" (Deuteronomy 5:19), to land rights. To steal a man's land is to deprive him of his patrimony, and to drive his family into starvation.

Pastoral people like the Bedouin are able easily to mark their pasturing territories by natural topographical features. By contrast, farmers on the floodplain of a river like the Nile or Euphrates need to set up stone markers to reestablish the corners of their own land once the flood waters have subsided. Babylonians carved their boundary markers, called *Kudurru*, with bas-reliefs of god and of king, and with inscriptions identifying the owner, and cursing anyone who would remove or relocate the stone. One of the finest of such pieces, the *kudurru* of Marduk-apla-iddina, is on display at the Pergamon Museum in Berlin.

Property rights occupy a significant portion of the Code of Hammurabi. For example, line 55 reads, "If a man, upon opening his canal for irrigation, becomes so lazy that he has let water ravage a field adjoining his, he shall measure out grains on the basis of those adjoining his" (Ibid. Pritchard, p. 168). Only when boundary markers are set and fixed can such a claim be adjudicated.

Those who purposely violated a neighbor's property could incur even more severe penalties. A tablet from the Assyrian capital city of Asshur contains the edict, "If a nobleman has encroached on the more important bounded property of his neighbor, when they have prosecuted him and convicted him, he shall give up one-third as much field as he encroached on; they shall cut off one finger of his; they shall flog him one hundred (times) with staves (and) he shall do the work of the king for one full month" (Ibid. Pritchard, p. 186).

"Cursed be he who misleads a blind man" (Deuteronomy 27:18). To clarify the eighth commandment against bearing false witness (Deuteronomy 5:20), Deuteronomy propagates two more new pieces of legislation. First, in the fourth curse (vs. 18), the Mosaic code forbids giving false directions to anyone about the unseen road ahead in their lives. Leviticus already legislated against two acts of violence against the disabled: "You shall not curse the deaf or put a stumbling block before the blind" (Leviticus 19:14). Now, Deuteronomy extends the provision to cover harmful untruths as well. To direct a blind man to walk unknowingly off a cliff would be the most perverse kind of lie and a form of murder as well.

The fifth curse picks up an important Deuteronomic theme, "Cursed be he who perverts the justice due to the sojourner, the fatherless, and the widow" (Deuteronomy 27:19). Already the book extended to "the sojourner, the fatherless, and the widow" the right to receive support, along with the priests, from the Hebrew tithe (Deuteronomy 14:29). That was mercy, but here the same book speaks of justice. Among the most perverse scoundrels on the face of the earth are those who would defraud a widow or cheat an orphan of his patrimony. The Code of Hammurabi shares this concern with the rights of inheriting minors and widows. Those who would appear in court and perjure themselves through the falsification of wills or other records, for the purpose of denying justice to the needy, are guilty of both lying and theft, and if their actions lead to the early death of their victims, they are also guilty of murder.

The prophets and apostles continue to develop this Deuteronomic theme of solicitude for the rights of the needy. The prophet Jeremiah laments: "They know no bounds in deeds of wickedness; they judge not with justice the cause of the fatherless, to make it prosper, and they do not defend the rights of the needy" (Jeremiah 5:28). The prophet Zechariah teaches the people: "Render true judgments, and show kindness and mercy each to his brother, do not oppress the widow, the fatherless, the sojourner, or or the poor; and let none of you devise evil against his brother in your heart" (Zechariah 7:9–10). And in the New Testament, the Apostle Saint James instructs: "Religion that is pure and undefiled before God and the Father is this: to visit orphans and widows in their affliction, and to keep oneself unstained from the world" (James 1:27).

"Cursed be he who slays his neighbor in secret" (Deuteronomy 27:24). To the fifth commandment against killing (Deuteronomy 5:17), two more curses add specificity against secret murders and murder for hire (Deuteronomy 27:24–25). Of course, to kill in broad daylight is wrong, but murder at night adds an element of cowardice that is particularly revolting. In ancient and medieval times, right up to the Old West, the honorable way of settling a dispute between men was through armed combat or a gunfight. Only a coward would stab a man in the back. Similarly, the frontier code looked down upon the paid killer, as someone doing a coward's dirty work for him.

"Cursed be he who does not confirm the words of this law by doing them" (Deuteronomy 27:26). The eighth and final curse addresses itself to the global obligation of the people to the whole Torah. They are not to pick and choose, following one law and not another. Their bond is to the legislation as the whole, and not just to each of the parts, for the Torah has to do with their unitary relationship to Almighty God. There should be a corresponding blessing, something like, "Blessed be he who confirms the words of this law by doing them." No doubt such a blessing existed, and was recited from Mount Gerizim, but the text of it has disappeared, while only the curse recited from Ebal remains.

For Saint Paul, this final curse epitomizes the inadequacy of the Torah, despite all its excellence. "For all who rely on works of the law are under a curse; for it is written, 'Cursed be every one who does not abide by all things written in the book of the law, and do them.' Now it is evident that no man is justified before God by the law; for 'He who through faith is righteous shall live;' but the law does not rest on faith, for 'He who does them shall live by them.' Christ redeemed us from the curse of the law, having become a curse for us—for it is written, 'Cursed be every one who hangs on a tree'—that in Christ Jesus the blessing of Abraham might come upon the Gentiles, that we might receive the promise of the Spirit through faith" (Galatians 3:10–14).

Saint Paul seems to be of two minds towards the Torah. Despite the contrast that he propounds between the Torah and the Gospel, he continues to draw upon materials from the Torah in all of his writings. In fact, his epistolarly corpus comprises one vast commentary on the Torah. Take, for example, his treatment of a beautiful passage from Chapter 30 of Deuteronomy:

It is not in heaven, that you should say, "Who will go up for us to heaven, and bring it to us, that we may hear it and do it?" Neither is it beyond the sea, that you should say, "Who will go over the sea for us, and bring it to us, that we may hear it and do it?" But the word is very near you; it is in your mouth and in your heart, so that you can do it. Deuteronomy 30:12–14	Moses writes that the man who practices the righteousness which is based on the law shall live by it. But the righteousness based on faith says, Do not say in your heart, "Who will ascend into heaven?" (that is to bring Christ down) or "Who will descend into the abyss?" (that is to bring Christ up from the dead). But what does it say? The word is near you, on your lips and in your heart (that is the word of faith which we preach); because, if you confess with your lips that Jesus is Lord and believe in your heart that God raised him from the dead, you will be saved. Romans 10:5–8

What Paul does here is to pit one Mosaic quotation against another. In refuting a law-based religiosity, Paul quotes from the Torah! In so doing, he practices an ancient rabbinic technique called *Gezerah Sheba,* bringing together two quotations from the Torah (or from the Prophets), to elucidate a text or a theological point.

If the Torah, in the form in which it has come down to us, contains curses that are more explicit than blessings, the implied blessings are easily enough discovered. Jesus reveals exactly that, when He pronounces the Beatitudes at the beginning of the Sermon on the Mount (Matthew 5:3–11). Jesus pronounces eight blessings that reverse the curses imposed by the world upon the poor, the mourning, the meek, the hungry, the merciful, the pure, the peaceable, the persecuted, and those sent by God. In so doing, Jesus does not abolish the Torah, but fulfills it (Matthew 5:18).

> Blessed are the poor in spirit, for theirs is the kingdom of heaven.
> Blessed are those who mourn, for they shall be comforted.
> Blessed are the meek, for they shall inherit the earth.
> Blessed are those who hunger and thirst for righteousness,
>   for they shall be satisfied.
> Blessed are the merciful, for they shall obtain mercy.
> Blessed are the pure in heart, for they shall see God.
> Blessed are the peacemakers, for they shall be called sons of God.
> Blessed are those who are persecuted for righteousness sake,
>   for theirs is the kingdom of heaven.
> Blessed are you when men revile you and persecute you and utter all kinds of evil
>   against you falsely on my account. Rejoice and be glad, for your reward is
>   great in heaven, for so men persecuted the prophets who were before you.
>   Matthew 5:3-11

1. What must Israel do in entering the Promised Land? Deuteronomy 27:1–13

2–3. List the twelve curses in Deuteronomy 27:15–26.

Deuteronomy 27:15	*Cursed be anyone who makes a false idol.*
Deuteronomy 27:16	
Deuteronomy 27:17	
Deuteronomy 27:18	
Deuteronomy 27:19	
Deuteronomy 27:20	
Deuteronomy 27:21	
Deuteronomy 27:22	
Deuteronomy 27:23	
Deuteronomy 27:24	
Deuteronomy 27:25	
Deuteronomy 27:26	

4. Write the blessing pronounced in Deuteronomy 28:3–6.

5. List some of the blessings of obedience found in Deuteronomy 28:7–14.

6–7. Explain some results from disobedience.

Deuteronomy 28:15–19	
Deuteronomy 28:20–29	
Deuteronomy 28:30–35	
Deuteronomy 28:36–37	
Deuteronomy 28:38–48	
Deuteronomy 28:49–57	
Deuteronomy 28:58–62	
Deuteronomy 28:63–68	

8. Explain the leading and providence in the desert. Deuteronomy 29:1–8

9. What comes before obedience to the covenant?

Deuteronomy 29:3–8	
CCC 368	

10. How can you set your heart on choosing God's will and obeying God's Word? Memorize Proverbs 4:23 if you need help in this area.

11. Find the warning for the sin discussed in Deuteronomy 29:15–20.

12. List some contemporary sources of idolatry.

13. Describe God's punishment for infidelity. Deuteronomy 29:21–28

14. What can you learn from the following passages?

Deuteronomy 30:6	
Jeremiah 4:4	
Hosea 10:12	
Romans 2:25–29	

15. What can you learn about the nature of God from the following verses?

Deuteronomy 30:1–10	
1 Kings 8:33–40	
Psalm 103:8–14	
CCC 210–211	
CCC 270	

16. Is there a particular time in your life when you repented and tasted God's mercy? Was there a time when you committed your heart and your life to God?

17. Are God's commands too difficult to understand? Deuteronomy 30:11–15

18. What choice is set before Israel? Deuteronomy 30:15–20

19. Why are your choices important? CCC 1696

20. Share a time in your life when you made a choice, a positive moral decision, which resulted in blessings for you and/or your loved ones.

CHAPTER 22

Moses on Mount Nebo
Deuteronomy 31–34

**Be strong and of good courage, do not fear or be in dread of them:
for it is the LORD your God who goes with you;
he will not fail you or forsake you.**
Deuteronomy 31:6

Religious Experience — At the heart of every religion is religious experience — starting with the experience of the religious founder. So Buddhism begins with the experience of Buddha, Islam with the experience of Muhammad, Christianity with the experience of Jesus Christ, Judaism with the experience of Moses.

When Moses saw the bush burning continually in the desert, he knew that something divine was happening. He was told to remove his sandals because the place was holy ground. The question was: Holy to whom?

Back in Egypt, Moses had become familiar with many false gods as well as the True One. His Hebrew family taught him about the God of Abraham, Isaac, and Jacob, and his Egyptian family told him about the god of Akhenaten, who had attempted to overthrow the many gods of Egypt in favor of just one god. By Moses' time, polytheism had returned with a vengeance, and all the shrines of the one god in Egypt had been destroyed. So Moses knew about Osiris, the god of the underworld, and about his brother Seth who had killed Osiris and was patron of the Nineteenth Dynasty. Moses knew about Isis, wife of Osiris, about Amun-Ra, the god of the sun, and about Ptuh, the god of wisdom. There was a canine-headed god, a feline-shaped goddess, a horned bovine goddess, and many other false gods.

So when Moses encountered the Divine in the desert, the uppermost question in his mind was not how the bush kept burning without being consumed. Modern commentators tend to focus on the physical aspect of the encounter. One theory suggests that the bush was over a petroleum deposit, so the bush acted like the wick of a candle! Talk about missing the point!

Moses never asked God: how are you doing this trick? Instead Moses wanted to know: Who are you? This was another way of asking, which god are you? Are you one of the many gods or are you The One? What relief Moses must have experienced when God told him, "I AM WHO AM."

How happy Moses must have been to meet the God who had revealed Himself to his ancestors Abraham, Isaac, and Jacob. Moses had already turned his back on Egypt and her false gods, and now the true God showed His face to Moses.

Later Moses brought the people of Israel back to the holy mountain in the desert, so that they could share in his religious experience there. The religious experience of Moses is foundational for three great religions, Judaism, Christianity, and Islam, all of which accept Moses as a true prophet. All of these three great religions also assert the validity of God's revelation to Moses. Over half the people on the face of the earth acknowledge the words that God actually spoke to Moses.

"He will not fail you or forsake you" (Deuteronomy 31:6). The early church took a profound interest in the final days of Moses, as well as the final days of Jesus. Both Moses and Jesus foresaw their deaths and gave careful instructions to their followers. The Jewish Christians of the First Century made constant cross-references between the two valedictory addresses, the farewell address of Moses to the twelve tribes of Israel, and the farewell of Jesus to the twelve apostles.

Moses, like Jesus after him, assures his followers that his own death is not a sign of divine disfavor. Whereas before they could look upon the face of Moses as one who had seen God and spoken to Him, after the death of Moses the people will have to continue on the basis of the Torah which God bequeathed to them through Moses. Therefore Moses says, "Be strong and of good courage, for it is the LORD your God who goes with you; he will not fail you or forsake you" (Deuteronomy 31:6). The continuing presence of the inspired Word of God will be a practical and efficacious grace in the life of the People of God.

As Moses left behind the Torah, Jesus left behind the Gospel, which inspires and challenges those called to participate in the life of the People of God. Also, God provides the grace to live the Gospel—"He will not fail you." The author of the Book of Hebrews, quoting Deuteronomy, points to both one of the challenges of the Gospel and to God's provision: "Keep your life free from love of money, and be content with what you have" (Hebrews 13:5). This verse is one of many sources for the Christian teaching of detachment from the things of this world. "He will not fail you" because He has already put His word into your heart.

"Then Moses spoke the words of this song" (Deuteronomy 31:30). Back in the Book of Exodus, Moses and the whole people sang a beautiful canticle after they passed through the Red Sea dry-shod (Exodus 15:1–18). Now, forty years later, Moses sings another, powerful canticle more than twice as long (Deuteronomy 32:1–43). The Exodus canticle praised the Lord for the miracle by which the people were saved while their enemies were punished for trying to destroy them; the Deuteronomy canticle is a monotheistic reflection, a more abstract consideration of the nature of the true God and the punishment in store for those who worship false gods. In the first canticle the Egyptians had been the enemy, but in the latter canticle the danger comes from within, from the forgetfulness of the people about their covenant relationship with God (Deuteronomy 32:18).

"Vengeance is mine, and recompense" (Deuteronomy 32:35). Deuteronomy chapter 32 is the original source for the proverb, "Vengeance is mine, I will repay, says the LORD"

(Romans 12:19). Saint Paul added those words "says the Lord" when he quoted the proverb from Deuteronomy in his Letter to the Romans. The Letter to the Hebrews also quotes this passage (Hebrews 10:30), but without adding the extra words. These New Testament commentaries find in the passage a precedent for the Christian doctrine of forgiveness. Since God alone is judge of the world, God alone has the right to decide who shall be rewarded and who shall be punished. Human vengeance preempts the divine prerogative. When we take vigilante action against each other, we ourselves become rebels against God.

Vengeance is mine, and recompense for the time when their foot shall slip; for the day of their calamity is at hand, and their doom comes swiftly. For the LORD will vindicate his people and have compassion on his servants, when he sees that their power is gone, and there is none remaining, bond or free. Deuteronomy 32:35–36	Repay no one evil for evil, but take thought for what is noble in the sight of all. If possible, so far as it depends upon you, live peaceably with all. Beloved, never avenge yourselves, but leave it to the wrath of God; for it is written, "Vengeance is mine, I will repay, says the LORD." No, "if your enemy is hungry, feed him; if he is thirsty, give him drink; for by so doing you will heap burning coals upon his head." Do not be overcome by evil but overcome evil with good. Romans 12:17–21	A man who has violated the law of Moses dies without mercy at the testimony of two or three witnesses. How much worse punishment do you think will be deserved by the man who has spurned the Son of God, and profaned the blood of the covenant by which he was sanctified and outraged the Spirit of grace? For we know him who said, "Vengeance is mine, I will repay." And again, "The LORD will judge his people." It is a fearful thing to fall into the hands of the living God. Hebrews 10:28–31

"Ascend this mountain of the Abarim, Mount Nebo" (Deuteronomy 32:49). The noble deaths of Moses and Jesus can, and do, speak eloquently to all people and not just to those of Jewish origin. Moses died on Mount Nebo within sight of the Promised Land. Jesus died on Mount Calvary, preparing to open the gates of heaven. We will each someday find ourselves on a personal Mount Nebo, where we hope to enjoy the grace of Christ won on Mount Calvary. Jesus will be our Savior, and Moses too will be our help, along with the rest of the saints and angels.

For Saint Peter, for example, his Mount Nebo was the Vatican Hill in Rome, where he was crucified upside down in the Circus of Nero as part of Nero's persecution of the early Christians. For Saint Pius X, Blessed John XXIII, and Pope John Paul II, as for so many successors of Saint Peter, their Mount Nebo was one and the same, a small papal apartment overlooking Saint Peter's Square in Rome.

Every point on the face of the earth is the same to God, who is not bound by time or space. Wherever Nebo may prove to be, the same words may be heard: "Come, O blessed of my Father, inherit the kingdom prepared for you from the foundation of the world" (Matthew 25:34).

"No man knows the place of his burial" (Deuteronomy 34:6). The Hebrews took care to preserve the tombs of their ancestors. Abraham had purchased a field near Hebron with a natural cave suitable for burials (Genesis 23:9); "There they buried Abraham and Sarah his wife; there they buried Isaac and Rebekah his wife" (Genesis 49:31). The sons of Jacob conveyed the body of their father in solemn procession from the land of Egypt to be buried next to his wife Leah in the family tomb at Hebron (Genesis 50:13).

Since the Holy Land was already in sight upon the death of Moses, one wonders why the Hebrews did not convey his body to Hebron to be joined to those of the patriarchs. They were bringing the bones of the patriarch Joseph with them for reburial in the Land (Exodus 13:19). According to ancient Jewish tradition, Joseph's bones found their final resting place not at Hebron, but at Shechem, in the shadow of Mount Gerizim. Joseph's mother Rachel herself was buried elsewhere also, where she died on the road near Bethlehem.

So it was that Moses, the man of God, who was raised in the house of Pharaoh, and challenged one of the most powerful pharaohs in the long history of Egypt, ended up with no funeral monument, not even a simple stone. He left behind, however, a monument greater than the pyramids, the powerful spiritual legacy of the Torah. When the last of the pyramids is reduced to sand, the teachings of Moses will continue to be living and active, for they constitute the Word of God.

"Two men talked with Him, Moses and Elijah" (Luke 9:30). Twelve hundred years after his death, Moses makes a surprise reappearance in the New Testament narratives of the Transfiguration of Jesus. Two great prophets of the Old Testament, Moses and Elijah, appear alongside Jesus conversing with Him at the moment of Transfiguration. Matthew and Luke mention Moses first with the sequence "Moses and Elijah" (Matthew 17:3, Luke 9:30), while Mark gives Elijah the first honor within the sequence "Elijah with Moses" (Mark 9:4).

Matthew and Mark simply mention that Moses and Elijah were speaking with Jesus, but Luke reveals the topic of the conversation: "And behold, two men talked with him, Moses and Elijah, who appeared in glory and spoke of his departure, which he was to accomplish in Jerusalem" (Luke 9:30). Moses and Elijah had spectacular departures of their own, Moses climbing the mountain to view the Promised Land, and Elijah ascending to heaven in a fiery chariot. They very nearly transcended death in their own persons, and so prefigured the perfect transcendence achieved by the Risen Christ.

1. How long did Moses live? Deuteronomy 31:1–2

2. Who will lead the Chosen People to the Promised Land? Deuteronomy 31:3–8

3. What words of advice are given in the following passages?

Deuteronomy 31:6	
Hebrews 13:5	

4. How did Moses know he was dying? Deuteronomy 31:14–16

5. After Moses finished writing, where was the law? Deuteronomy 31:24–26

6. Contrast the following passages.

Deuteronomy 32:5–6	
Philippians 2:14–16	

7. What does the term "son of God" signify?

Deuteronomy 32:8–9	
CCC 441	

8. What can you learn from the following passages?

Deuteronomy 32:35–36	
Romans 12:17–21	
Hebrews 10:28–31	

9. Can you recall a situation in which you repaid an evil done to you with good?

10. What can you learn about the prime mover in the course of history?

Deuteronomy 32:39	
Isaiah 45:5–7	
Sirach 11:14	
CCC 304	

* God is the Lord of history. Is God the Lord of your life? Could you prove it?

11. Why can you call God "Father?"

Deuteronomy 32:43–47	
Hebrews 1:5–6	
CCC 238	

12. Why should you know and obey the law?

Deuteronomy 32:44-47	
CCC 2056	

13–14. Find the praise or blessing that Moses gave to the tribes of Israel.

Deuteronomy 33:6	
Deuteronomy 33:7	
Deuteronomy 33:8–11	
Deuteronomy 33:12	
Deuteronomy 33:13–17	
Deuteronomy 33:18–19	
Deuteronomy 33:20–21	
Deuteronomy 33:22	
Deuteronomy 33:23	
Deuteronomy 33:24–25	

15. In what ways do contemporary people forget God (Deuteronomy 32:18)?
List some practical ways that help you keep God in your thoughts.

16. What can you say about Moses? Sirach 45:1–5

17. How old was Moses when he died? What was his health? Deuteronomy 34:7

18. Where is Moses buried? Deuteronomy 34:6

19. Describe Joshua. Deuteronomy 34:9

20. Why is Moses considered a great prophet? Deuteronomy 34:10–12

* Moses blessed the tribes of Israel. Recall a virtuous trait of each person in your small group (or in your family) and then, in writing, or aloud, share a way in which each person has been a blessing to you.

The Exodus

Wandering in the Desert
on the way
to the Promised Land

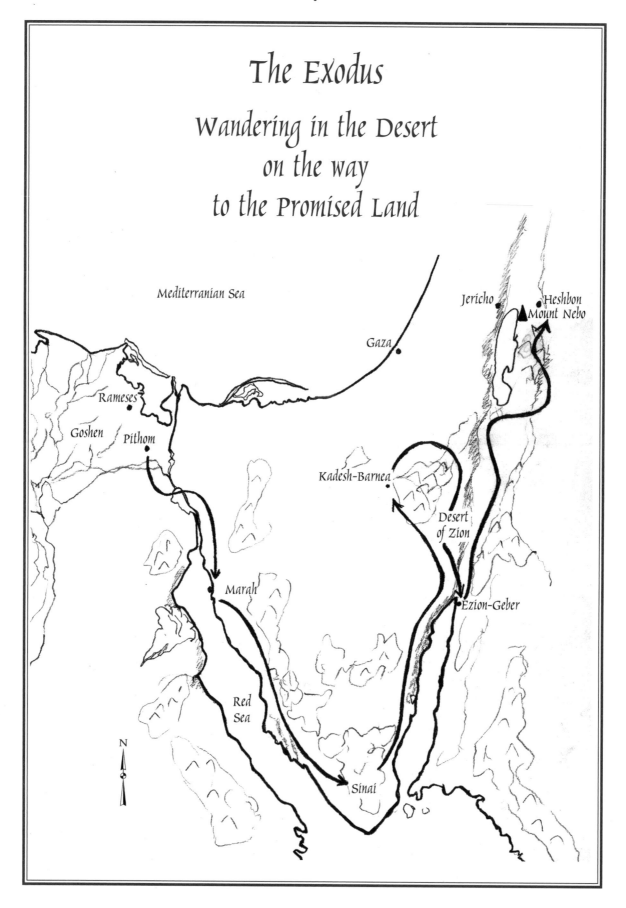

Mediterranian Sea

Jericho

Heshbon
Mount Nebo

Gaza

Rameses

Goshen

Pithom

Kadesh-Barnea

Desert
of Zion

Marah

Ezion-Geber

Red
Sea

N

Sinai